Various contributing authors

authorHOUSE®

AuthorHouse™
1663 Liberty Drive
Bloomington, IN 47403
www.authorhouse.com
Phone: 1-800-839-8640

Published by AuthorHouse   12/05/2012

ISBN: 978-1-4772-9493-2 (sc)
ISBN: 978-1-4772-9492-5 (e)

Library of Congress Control Number: 2012922596

This book is printed on acid-free paper.

Contents

Introduction, *Frank Wiederrecht*............................ 1

Blessed, *Frank Wiederrect*.. 5

A Long Walk Home, *Jerry Kinner*............................. 11

What A Friend We Have, *Shirley Blakeley* 17

Because He First Loved Us, *Kendra Jamerman*................ 23

Always Forgiven, *Rachel McGee* 27

Heart And Soul, *Gene Ragland* 35

Never An Instantaneous Event, *Sue Ragland*................. 41

Painful Reality—Personal Relationship, *Linda Carlat*....... 47

In God We Trust, *Shelagh (Wisdom) Basso* 55

The Light As It Shines, *Carolee Hornbuckle* 63

Bandage The Hurt, Heal The Sick, Find The Lost,

    Deb Gorsuch... 71

Fully Forgiven, Fully Forgiving, *Ginger Baumann* 79

Just Show Up, *Pat Baumann* 87

Close Encounters Of The Godly Kind, *Pat Bledsoe* 93

Be Still And Know, *Susan Foley*.............................. 101

Let Go, Let God, *Sharon Jensen* 109

See That He Is Good, *Monty Jensen* 117

Always Enough, *Sharon Taylor* 127

Never An Accident, *Dick Taylor* 133

Spiritually Discerned, *Liz Bartos* 141

The Mighty Hands Of God, *Francis J. Horn* 151

This book is dedicated
to all those who stand in the chain of faith
that begins with Jesus and His disciples and
faithfully travels through every generation
until the message of the gospel reaches us today.
We humbly stand in this chain of faith
hoping and praying that our contribution
will encourage generations after us to
"seek the Lord while He may be found."

About the Authors

The testimonies in *Gathering Faith* come from the diverse voices of everyday people that live real life on the windswept grasslands and hills of Wyoming. From their pens spill personal, intimate experiences that have changed their lives and the lives of friends and families.

Introduction

Frank Wiederrecht

The Gathering is a "church for people who don't do church." We have a non-churchy name, and meet in a non-churchy building, and worship in a non-churchy way to better reach people who are 'unchurched' or 'de-churched.'

If you were to visit one of our gatherings you would see people of every flavor and from every walk of life. A janitor, a state senator, a rancher, and maybe the mayor might be worshiping next to a young man sporting a Mohawk and ear plugs. An unwed teen mother and a Doctor of Education might be working together in the children's department. All would say that they are looking for reality, relevance, and relationship.

From the very beginning The Gathering has had as its intention that it would be 'A Safe Place for Spiritual Investigation, Formation, and Growth.' Words fail to express the depth of our emotions when we say this.

Faith, Religion, Churches and Denominations have proven themselves over and over again to be unsafe for many of us who really just want a relationship with Jesus. When we've not believed right, behaved better, worshipped correctly, or looked nice (and the list goes on and on), we have—in one way or another—been shown the door. This is not an unusual or uncommon experience for our people. When I have asked for a show of hands as to who all have been hurt at one time or another by religion or religious people, ninety-nine percent have raised their hands.

It was said of Jesus that he was a 'friend of sinners and tax collectors and that 'many followed him.' Now the religious stuffed-shirts of his day absolutely couldn't understand why a young up-and-coming rabbi like Jesus would want to tarnish his reputation by hanging around 'people like that,' but He said *it isn't the healthy who need a doctor.*

In 2005 a group of 'outcasts and misfits' decided to start a 'church for the rest of us.' We know that we are sick and need a doctor; we know that we are sinful and need a savior! The question is not if we are good enough to be 'church people' but rather 'is there any hope for the likes of us?' And to that question we've heard Jesus give a resounding **YES!**

We understand that real people have real problems, and really need God's love and intervention. We made the decision that we would talk about real things that really matter. Now, we have decided to share our stories with each other. And that is how this book came into being.

We do not believe that our stories are all that unusual or sensational, but instead—representative—of people all over our nation and the world. What might be a bit unusual is the willingness to get up on a Sunday morning and tell the world what a sinner you've been.

But we are tired of faking it. We are tired of ignoring it. We **want** reality. We are okay with knowing and being known by the extent of God's grace in our lives. We believe that people—maybe someone like you—is still interested enough to ask, *does faith really work for some people, and could it work for me?*

We sincerely hope so!

Reaching out is what we do, and what we love. We invite you to visit our website at www.thegatheringdouglas.com. There, you can view what The Gathering is all about, view photos, events, and even enjoy videos of messages.

It is with great delight that we share a sampling of stories from The Gathering's down-to-earth parishioners. Please read on!

Pastor Frank Wiederrecht
Douglas, Wyoming

Blessed

Frank Wiederrect

I was born on a farm in Iowa and our family always attended Sunday School and church. I sang in the choir with my dad and read the scripture from the lectern. I was a good church boy on the weekend, but gained a real foul mouth the rest of the time. I was never allowed to go to parties, but wanted to. So again, I thought I was better than the 'party kids,' yet if given half a chance, I'd have been one of them.

From my early years, I gained a respect for God and the Bible, but for me back then God was a subject to be studied, not a person to be known. I said prayers all the time: the Lord's Prayer, prayers before meals, prayers at bedtime, but I wasn't really praying. I was reciting prayers from rote. I can't really say that I had a faith at this time—I had religious practices.

I went to college, and for the first time I was away from my parent's direct influence and control. Like many kids, I experimented with alcohol and marijuana. Beer made me sick and the weed didn't do anything for me except taste bad. I had a girlfriend and would have headed down the wrong road there, but just before getting over-involved, some guys from my dorm floor invited me to join a Bible Study. I'd never ever seriously studied the Bible. Amazingly, in the churches I'd attended, we didn't study the Bible. I felt that this would be a great opportunity to do so. These guys asked me what I thought a 'Christian' was. I told them that it was *someone who follows the teachings of Jesus Christ.* Then they asked me who Jesus was to me. I told them *that I really don't know.* They drew out a simple illustration of how we are separated from God because of our sins and that Jesus is the God / Man who is the bridge between heaven and earth and the means by which we reconnect with God.

I don't remember everything about that night, but I do remember two things: whenever I asked a question, they could turn to chapter and verse and answer all my questions directly from the Bible. I'd never known anyone who could do that. Second, when they prayed—they were talking to a person (God) who they knew and loved personally. It was evident that they knew God!

I remember crying, overwhelmed by their faith and love for God and wanting that myself. On October 8, 1974, in my dorm room, I asked Jesus to forgive my sins and to make me into the person He created me to be. Immediately, my mouth changed. I no longer used curse words. I also (after several attempts) broke up with my girlfriend. I began attending a church made up of 'Jesus People'—hippy looking college students. We'd sit around discussing the Bible during Sunday School and then in the worship service, we'd sing Jesus songs accompanied by guitars, keys and drums.

I was baptized in a lake two years after giving my life to Jesus. I also met my future wife at that church. Ann was the lead keyboard player and singer for the *Good News Singers*, a Jesus-type Jazz choir affiliated with the church.

Previously I had been an Engineering major, but after giving my life to Christ, I felt God's call to serve Him vocationally. I ended up majoring in Anthropology and Religion, as well as becoming a Christian leader on Campus and in my church. I actually became an intern at the church and married Ann there.

Eventually I felt God's call to go to seminary (grad school for pastors). It was during that time that we began to see that our pastor, who was so great in many ways, was also very controlling in many others. He'd tell us what kind of car to buy and where to work and give us permission to date or marry. That was too extreme for us, especially since I had visited six different seminaries around the country and decided to go to one in Texas. Since the Pastor didn't agree with that one he wouldn't give me a recommendation to go there.

Ann and I decided to leave that church. We also found out that if you left, when you left—you were actually kicked out. Our friends, who had been our friends all through college—even our best man and bridesmaid—had to 'shun' us, or turn their backs toward us. They were to ignore our presence, not take our calls, and pretend we were dead.

That hurt us badly, but we started attending another church where we learned God's grace for the very first time. We joined there, and were given a recommendation to attend the seminary I had felt called to. That ended up being a mixed blessing.

When I first came to Christ, I experienced his leading each and every day. I believed God was talking to me and guiding me. But the seminary I attended didn't believe that God did that today. It was a very 'heady' time. I learned to translate the Bible out of the original Hebrew and Greek texts. I became very 'studious' during this time. I didn't lose my relationship with God, but it sure changed from being real personal to being more 'intellectual.'

I remember that I had three professors who were different. They knew God and when they prayed for us students—it seemed as if heaven itself opened. I praise God for these guys, but still felt that I fell short of the mark of what they had. I graduated and became an associate pastor for three years and then a denominational pastor for seventeen years. During most of that time, I was confused. I was confused about what the normal Christian life was supposed to be. I was confused that many 'Christians' could be so mean and controlling. I was confused about where I was supposed to minister, because I never seemed to 'fit' anywhere. I tried real hard to 'bloom where you're planted.'

Sometimes God leads in mysterious ways. We started The Gathering (a church for people who don't do church) and from the very beginning and along every step of the way, God has been more real to me than ever! I am learning to truly sit back and watch God work! I don't have to play politics. I don't have to pretend to be someone I'm not. I truly am learning to 'do life with God.' I expect God to show up at our services and **He *does***! I expect God to be at work in all our lives and **He *is***!

I praise God for all the changed lives that I get to see, and that I get to do life and ministry with my friends and family at The Gathering. It is a truly life-giving experience for me and my family! I am blessed!

A Long Walk Home

Jerry Kinner

My entire life has been a pilgrimage, both physically and spiritually. I've lived all over the West and southwest working for the telephone company, and attended every sort of church imaginable, but I really didn't know what I was searching for.

As a youth I attended a community church (The Little Log Church on the hill.) We lived on a ranch and sometimes could not attend because of bad weather or ranch duties. Even though I attended church, I didn't think about God much. I was just busy being a kid and didn't give it a lot of deep thought. I always tried to be a good and honest kid, and I believed that was what it was all about. Looking back, I remember my grandmother always tried to encourage me in spiritual things, and even though I agreed with her I didn't always follow her advice. Grandma knew the Lord, and she was the most positive person I knew at that time. She beamed with the love of God all the time.

When I turned fourteen we left the ranch. I attended church, but rarely. There was a fundamentalist church about a block away, and on Sunday I could hear the preacher yelling at the top of his lungs all about sin. I formed an aversion to fundamentalism. Another time I went with a friend to his church and while I was in the service, my dad sent my sister in to drag me out.

When we moved to Colorado Springs, Colorado, we began attending a mainline church. I joined the youth fellowship group where we had Bible study but I mostly went to participate in the games we played afterwards. In all honesty, I never gave much thought to Christ and his promise.

Right out of high school I was hired on by the telephone company as an installer. Sheila and I were married when I was nineteen and she was sixteen. We went to church very sporadically. We sometimes attended liberal churches, as the others we found were too strict. We were told at some of those churches that if you were not a member, you were not saved.

At the time I also had a problem with the idea of it being necessary to be born again, so I kept away from any church that preached that particular message. My job required moving constantly, sometimes as often as once a week, so for many years we didn't even attend a church. We lived in a mobile home that I towed behind my 1953 GMC pickup, and without roots it was easy to have many more things to keep us busy. Once again, God got left in our dust.

I never had a taste of liquor until I got out of high school, but in order to associate with my fellow workers, I began to visit the bars and frequent parties. That began to cause problems between Sheila and me and I eventually quit doing those things.

When we finally moved to Gillette in the hopes to become more settled, we knew we needed to attend a church, especially for our children. Both of us became quite involved and became Sunday school teachers. I became a Deacon and later elected as a Ruling Elder. I became rather proud of my accomplishments, and did a lot of work in the church: fund-raising (which I hated), distributing baskets on Thanksgiving and Christmas, and taking the local missionary preacher around to various rural churches. All this time I was thinking I was a very good Christian. I even gave a couple of sermons . . . but I still didn't really know Jesus.

Later, I was promoted to management in the telephone company. The advancement developed into a really stressful job. I would wake up with my jaw so tight I literally had to work to get my mouth open, and it never occurred to me to ask for the Lord's help.

In the spring of 1976 I moved to Douglas and oversaw a crew of fifteen people. Douglas was exploding with new housing and businesses so again, I became extremely stressed and eventually developed TMJ. I spent a year or more in braces to correct the problem. I was also a real worrier, and brought my work home with me at night. I ended up losing what little I knew about the peace of the Lord.

After we came to Douglas we attended a mainline church and became involved there. Sheila also opened a fabric shop, and I did double duty repairing sewing machines and continued to work for the telephone company.

In 1983 we bought our current home on fourth street and moved the store there. In time, we began building on. All of our spare time was spent working and we quit attending church, feeling that we didn't have time. We also had begun to feel that our church was getting much too liberal . . . one more excuse.

In 2004 Sheila was diagnosed with lung cancer. This became a two-year struggle with many hospital stays and various treatments. During that time Sheila was very confident that she would beat the cancer, but it was not to be. She became aware that she needed to be saved and I believe she was, through the work of my sister and brother-in-law, Roy (a minister and missionary) and Martha Wisner.

I lost the love of my life on June 26, 2006, after almost fifty-three years of marriage.

I still resisted the teachings and help of Roy and Martha, but the Lord was still working as I began to feel an emptiness and an unexplainable desire for spiritual fulfillment. I did not want to return to our old church and I still am not sure what led me to the door of The Gathering Place. I feel it had to be a 'God thing.' At The Gathering Place I finally discovered what I had been missing for so long, and I have gradually turned to Christ and accepted His great promise. The change in my life has been amazing. My mouth suddenly became clean and my stress level lower. I have started to give much more, time, money, and of myself. It has become easier for me to talk about Christ and what He has done for me.

It is amazing how, when I give my resources (which I never seemed to have enough of before), they seem to be more than enough. Yes, I still am a sinner and I struggle. I have a longing to grow more in Christ, and I still need all those at The Gathering and elsewhere to help me in this journey until I reach my eternal home, and never have to move again!

What A Friend We Have!

Shirley Blakeley

Looking back over the years from the vantage point of a senior citizen and in view of what my faith has meant to me, there are some things I would do differently. For instance, I would not rely on the church to define who God is to me. I would be much more diligent and less selfish in my prayer life. I would seek His guidance in both major and daily decisions.

I received salvation at the age of eleven, and maintained a deep interest in religion and God. I read accounts of people who were healed, had tangible answers to prayers and claimed to be a friend of God. But all of that seemed unreal to me. *Did people just make this stuff up?* None of that had been a part of my experience, and I held God at arm's length. I felt the need to attend church in order to truly become close to God, but there wasn't one in the rural area where I lived for twenty-six years. I read my Bible (with little understanding) and argued with friends the advantages and disadvantages of a belief in God. I never got to know God in a personal way—as a *friend*. During that part of my life God was someone far away—to be looked at—to be studied—but not to *know*.

My niece took her own life when she was twenty-one. It was then I began to really ponder the meaning of life. She had attempted suicide several times before, and in my desperation to understand the 'why?' I hungered to bring God closer. I wanted to make Him a much larger part of my life, and to understand Him and the reasons why He allowed things to happen. I didn't know how. I realized that *I* needed to become closer to *Him*, and I thought back to the day I gave my life to Christ when I was a child. Still, truly understanding Him seemed so very far away.

When a church finally established in our area I rushed to it, believing that it was my answer for finding God. To say I was disappointed is an understatement. It never occurred to me at the time that the church wasn't always where God was, and I continued living life without seeking His guidance. All the while I was asking *why would He be concerned with my little life?*

There were times when I would have the feeling that what I was doing wasn't quite right, but I never thought to talk to God about it. Prayer for me then consisted of pleading for things—material things—and asking Him to make certain people behave in the way I wanted them to behave. Needless to say, my prayers were mostly unanswered and I felt even further removed from God.

Even though I felt a great distance from God during that time, He blessed me with two extraordinary children. If ever I knew for certain my prayers were answered it was in the lives of my children. When they were teenagers I knew I could not be with them and protect them as I had when they were little, so I gave them over to God and prayed daily for His guidance and protection for them. He has been faithful in His promise to guide and protect—I can see it in their lives in the exceptional people they have chosen to marry and in the five wonderful grandchildren they have produced.

When my children had grown I determined to further my education. No—I didn't seek God's guidance first (are you seeing a pattern here)? Because of my niece's suicide and the conflicted relationships I had experienced, I wanted to know more about what made people do the things they do. To that end I focused on social work and counseling. I earned my degrees and spent the next fifteen years being a sort of "paid friend" to lonely, hurting people. I was someone they could talk to, bare their souls to and not have to worry about whether I would speak to them again or not. I was, after all, being paid to listen.

In the course of time (oh, yes, I'm a slow learner) I saw that people were often helped just by having someone listen to their problems. I didn't always have the answers for them, but I could listen and help them see that the other people in their lives had their own problems . . . problems that could account for their actions, either good or bad.

As I listened to others I felt a void in my own life of the absence of having anyone who would listen to me and my problems. I was seen as the person who had all the answers, but I didn't. Not by a long shot.

At the same time it seemed that everything I read or heard about had to do with being a friend. I finally had to do some research on the word 'friend,' and one of the things I learned was that a root of the word 'friend' translates to 'free to love.' We love family members very often because we are expected to love them. But, a friend is someone that we are free to love . . . or not.

That knowledge had a profound effect on me—that simple knowledge that I was free to love the people I called my friends. It was then that I heard a song about being a friend of God. Later I read James 2:23 which refers to Abraham as being the friend of God.

God as my *friend* had a very different meaning for me than God as my *Father* (even though He is). A father can be stern, even frightening at times. But a *friend*—that's different, at least for me it was. I began to talk with God like I would talk to a friend. Since then our friendship has grown and I am learning new things every day about my friend. I am comforted knowing there is nothing I can't talk to Him about. After all He knows about it anyway. The world is a less lonely place because I have a friend who is always there for me.

Because He First Loved Us

Kendra Jamerman

I took on a lot of guilt, shame and anger towards God early in life. I was molested when I was seven years old. In my pain and suffering, I questioned _how could a loving father allow something like this to happen to an innocent child?_

God's word in Hebrews 13:5 says "I will never leave you nor forsake you."

Really? Where were you, Jesus? **_Where were you?_**

When I came to accept Christ as my personal Lord and Savior on January 29. 1990, I didn't really expect lightening bolts. But I expected to feel **something** different. I went on to serve and I tried to read the Bible. Eventually I became frustrated. I didn't get a whole lot from reading the old testament. In my mind it reinforced a belief that God was a distant, angry God who punished. I served because I believed that was what I was supposed to do.

I led a women's Bible study group and organized a woman's retreat. I became a children's church director, a nursery worker, a Christian woman's club director and a small group leader. I served on the church board and even brought in The Power Team.

Yet, no matter how hard I tried and no matter how hard I worked, I still didn't feel that much closer to God. I *did* grow in my walk with Christ, but there was a void that told me I was missing something. I wanted **Him** to use me in mighty ways. I wanted to feel **His** love for me, but I somehow couldn't. I wanted to love **Him**, but honestly—I just couldn't feel the connection.

People used to tell me that they couldn't wait to meet Jesus. I could. For one, I could never look Him in the eye. For two, I felt safer and more secure at a distance.

I recently had an experience that totally changed my life. It was an experience that was beyond my comfort zone, but I am truly a new person because of it. A friend invited me to a SOZO retreat, telling me that it was a healing encounter. I heard a Holy Spirit encounter and I wanted more of God. I went to the retreat.

God knew that if I heard healing, I never would have gone because I didn't think that I needed healing and I didn't want to dredge up the negative experiences and feelings from my past. What this encounter did was show me where God was during my time of sexual abuse. He was there the whole time with tears in his eyes, broken-hearted, waiting to take me by the hand and lead me out of the situation. But because of the shame that wasn't mine to begin with, I couldn't see Him. Because of that shame that I was never able to look Jesus in the eye and completely feel the love that He has for me. As a result, I could never completely love Him.

When I was finally able to cut the ties of that shame—to let Jesus take it from me—I saw a vision. It was a beam of light shining down on me in bed, covering me, and covering my exposure. Because of the shame, I had my back to that light.

When I was able to let go of that shame and give it to Him, I turned to face the light and saw Jesus standing at the door with His hand stretched out to mine. I reached out and grasped His hand, and He walked me through the door and away from all those years of guilt, shame, anger and abandonment.

I saw that He had not forsaken me! I immediately felt a wave of peace and contentment and for the first time, I was able to crawl up in Jesus' lap, look Him in the eye and see the sparkle of joy that He has for me!

And the love? The feeling of love that He has for me is so powerful and so strong that I never will leave it! And at last—*at last*—because I truly feel the love that He has for me, I am free to love Him completely! He has made me whole again. He has healed my broken heart. He has set me free!

1 John 4:19 says "We love because he first loved us". ***I get that!***

The bonus comes in reading my Bible. It is a special time that I look forward to every morning. The mental block that I had has disappeared, and that special time is my time to talk and listen to my savior. Reading His word is the only way that we get to know who He is, and the only way we can grow in our walk and our love for Him is by truly knowing Him!

I encourage you to search deep within your heart's hurts if you are having trouble finding Jesus. I promise you—***I promise you***—that he is there waiting for you to reach out to Him, and once you do, your life will ***never*** be the same!

Always Forgiven

Rachel McGee

$\mathcal{M}$y story about the development of my faith is the story of a journey. The journey has recently become quite clear to me. Each portion of my journey has been in response to great periods of distress and prayer. Ironically, those periods of prayer when God's answer came back, the result was a "no."

I don't remember a time in my life when I didn't believe that God was real. I was raised in a Lutheran Church in Minnesota and learned that pan cookies, coffee, casserole, Jello and Lutifisk were all part of the final supper, and should be partaken of regularly. It was only later in life that I realized Jesus and the disciples did not in fact share a meal of lime Jello with pears and tater-tot casserole.

I can recite the Kyrie, the Lord's prayer, the Apostle's Creed and a few others. But that was the greatest problem with the beginning of my journey. Nothing felt real . . . I knew that Jesus walked with me, but I sure didn't feel Him there. It was a lot of memorization without explanation. I knew my parents were believers, but we never talked about any of it. We only prayed out loud on holidays.

My high school youth group was the true beginning of my journey along with a dear, dear friend of mine. Her name was Cory. We talked about anything and everything. I went to Mexico on a mission trip with her church. I began to understand what being a Christ-follower really meant. But while all of these wonderful things started happening and my faith was growing, something else started as well. That was a feeling of not being 'good enough.'

It started as a glance in the mirror and thinking *I could lose a few pounds*. I somehow found my way to running. I started running in the winter of my sophomore year of high school, and ran excessively through the summer and fall. I started to lose weight; not a lot at first, just fifteen pounds or so. But the feelings of inadequacy got worse and not better. All of my friends had boyfriends and I thought I should as well. I continued to run and restrict what I ate. I continued to lose weight.

I ran in track my junior year. But no boyfriend. I assumed it was how I looked. I was taller than all my friends, and felt as though I was a giant. So I ran even more. I prayed daily that God would fix me and make me skinny. I was much more active in church and found rest there. I found rest in the Word. But I wasn't at rest with myself. *Why doesn't God fix me?*

I got to a dangerously low point of a hundred and fifteen pounds my senior year of high school. I hardly ate. I prayed a lot. I ran all the time. My quest to be thin had taken over my life. My track coach threatened to keep me from running on the team if I didn't gain back twenty pounds.

When my coach told me I couldn't run, I knew something was wrong. I turned to my boyfriend Tyler, and he admitted he didn't know what to do and couldn't handle it. He left. I managed to gain the weight and finish my track season, but felt worse than ever.

Despite my best attempts to lose the weight, I actually continued to gain weight through the summer. God answered that prayer with a "NO!" I knew that if I persevered, (Hebrews 12:1) that I would be successful. I knew God had a plan.

My freshman year of college was miserable. I continued to feel unworthy of love and affection, and at one point contemplated suicide. Well, God once again said "NO!" and I walked away from the window . . . never to return.

I made it through school that year. I ended up working at a Bible camp in Minnesota that summer. I realized that God had plans for me. I knew it was because the Lord carried me for a while, and I was able to make it through the anorexia and contemplation of suicide.

I was so excited at the revelation and realization of what faith can do, I wanted to share it with all my campers. I thought what better place to share such a wonderful story of hope and faith than Bible camp? I shared my story with one fifteen-year old. A couple of days later, the camp director told me that she was told that I had shared this story and that I was never do it again—it was too much. I felt shut down.

I began questioning God's purpose for me and wondering just what the heck He was thinking when he put me on this earth. I managed to get involved in a youth group back in Bemidji where I attended college, but never did I share my story. I prayed a lot that God would show me what he wanted me to do. I questioned whether my birth and placement on this earth was a mistake.

The following summer I decided to spend with my extended family in Illinois at their farm. There, I met a man and we began to date. My parents had moved to Arizona and my mom was teaching at the University of Arizona in the College of Nursing. As was my normal pre-school ritual, I went in for a physical. Having never had problems in the past, I figured I would breeze through with no problems.

Wrong again. I found out that I had an enlarged heart. After an echocardiogram and a trip to a cardiologist in Minneapolis, I was told I had a hole the size of a quarter between my atriums. By then, I was sleeping eighteen hours a day, and constantly felt exhausted and out of shape. My cardiologist said I was lucky—six months from a transplant.

I finally said "Yes God, I get it. You want me here! Next let's work on why!" It was an incredibly emotional time for me. I knew at that point that God ***did*** have big plans. He saved me, woke me up to my worth and again spent time carrying me. Unfortunately, it took me all that time to understand.

I made a full recovery from the open heart surgery. I transferred schools to be by my boyfriend, and we moved in together. All of these except the surgery turned out to be bad choices for me. To make a long story short, my boyfriend ended up being a verbally abusive alcoholic. I had prayed very long and hard that God would fix him and we would be okay. That was a 'no.' I didn't hesitate to leave the situation when my boyfriend tried to pin me down and choke me to death because I moved a plant. The moment I got myself free from his grip, I left.

God had much bigger plans for me than to die in that man's hands.

I graduated from college with a BS in Biology which I found out didn't get me far. My parents invited me to Arizona, and since my mom was teaching I could get a master's degree for a fraction of normal in state tuition. I was lucky enough to land a job with the Forest Service.

I had a lovely Mormon supervisor that decided it was unacceptable that I was twenty-three and unmarried. He set me up with a twenty-seven year old firefighter named Josh. We were married nine months later. That was almost ten years ago. Josh is the kindest, most sincere, and helpful man I know. He can even cut down a tree and save me from misplaced rattlesnakes! I am truly blessed to have him as my husband.

Less than two months after Josh and I were married, my mom passed away after a long, hard battle with Lupus. I knew that God had a reason to have taken her, and I no longer lived in despair. I knew God would get me through. I had faith that the pain would end, and I had hope that the sun would once again shine.

I knew had a teammate! Jesus walked next to me, and I was never alone. I always knew that no matter what life brought to me, God would get me through. I knew that I would be better and stronger for it. *"Rejoice in hope, be patient in suffering and persevere in prayer."* Romans 12:12

My faith has been tested and through each trial faith gets stronger. There may be times when I have forgotten, but God has been patient with me. I have always found my way back. Josh and I moved to Douglas almost three years ago. It was a tough move, and our workplace hasn't always been the easiest to work in. With patience and faith, I am beginning to see why I am here. I lost my father to prostate cancer just over a year ago. I knew I would eventually feel better and not so sad. God got me through—like always. No matter what

I face, I know that God is there for me. I have learned to stop asking for things my way, and to start listening to God's way.

I reached a point last winter where I was struggling with a friend who was not supportive during my grieving process. I prayed to God to show me what to do, and he led me to The Gathering. I cried the entire first service that I attended. I had found a home! God led me to a place that has helped me heal tremendously. I began attending First Place for Health Bible Study and through that I have truly begun to heal **all** of me. I have become involved in Youth Group and additional Bible studies. God continues to lead me down the road of peace.

I remember when I was in college that I wrote a poem that said "I am afraid that one day the bags I am carrying will be too much to bear." Well, I know now that I don't have to carry the weight of who I've been, because I am **forgiven**!

Heart And Soul

Gene Ragland

I am a recovering alcoholic. I was born with dyslexia, which was an unknown condition when I was young. Dyslexia makes words and sentences appear to be jammed up, backwards and confusing. Teachers and fellow students labeled me 'dumb' and 'stupid.'

I started drinking at a young age. Alcohol was easy to get and it was okay with my family, who were also drinkers. As I grew up I learned to get alcohol any way I could, even if I had to steal it or the money to get it. I had no conscience or morals for what I said or did. I was in a very "I" world, and if there was a God, I felt He never did anything for me—and that feeling went two ways.

Drinking did things for me that I could not do by myself. It made me good looking. It made me sing and play better. It made me dance better and it made me popular with the ladies. It made me six foot six and two hundred and eighty-five pounds. I was invincible—at least in my own head! It made me fit in so that I didn't feel like a loner.

In my teens I began to get into trouble with the law because of my drinking. I was seventeen when I got kicked out of school. When I had to appear in court, the judge gave me a choice: four years of reform school or the military. I joined the Navy.

My drinking increased and I ended up with three MIPs that I had acquired from the age of eighteen to twenty-one years old. The Navy got me out of all the charges all three times by telling the judges that I was just a kid learning to be a man, so I went unpunished.

Because of my drinking I started having blackouts and memory losses. The ship I was on went overseas a lot and I found I could drink anywhere else except in the US. When I was in France I turned twenty-one years old. My drinking increased even more.

Four months after I got out of the Navy I got married. We had two children—a boy and a girl. I continued to drink, and because of the drinking and then running around, my marriage only lasted four years. Self-pity and anger increased my drinking even more. Sometimes I would stay drunk for days or weeks. I pretty much drank from when I got up until I passed out at night. I didn't understand why I drank so much, but nothing changed.

In 1972, I met a nice lady and we got married. She had a six-year-old son and she gave me a son one year later. We were very much in love, but there still was no God in my life. Nothing changed. My drinking escalated even more. My family suffered and I started having blackouts most of the time.

I started playing the guitar and singing in a country band and that allowed me to drink for free. I thought that was cool, because I was 'in the band.' I didn't have to buy my own drinks! The bad part of that was being stopped by the law for drunk driving more than once. In 1987 I went in front of a judge for my fifth felony DUI, and again, I was given a choice: go to prison for seven to ten years, or go to Alcoholics Anonymous for help.

AA was my last chance. If I didn't get sober, the next charge I got would send me straight to prison.

I went to AA and a man there named Tommy became my sponsor. He had fifteen years of sobriety. He told me to go to as many meetings as I could, read the big book of AA and do the twelve steps. I went to four or five meetings a day, seven days a week for two years and I stayed sober. During those two years, I found a higher power called God! That made a huge difference in my ability to stay sober.

Tommy also told me that as I read the big book, I should look for my own story as I'd find it somewhere in those pages. I quote the words that seemed to relate to me: "Long since I had come to believe I was insane because I did so many things I didn't want to do. I didn't want to neglect my children. I loved them, I think, as much as any parent. But I did neglect them. I didn't want to get into fights, but I did get into fights. I didn't want to get arrested, but I did get arrested. I didn't want to jeopardize the lives of innocent people by driving an automobile while intoxicated, but I did. I quite naturally came to the conclusion that I must be insane." (Alcoholics Anonymous, 3rd Edition, 1976, paperback. p.199)

My sobriety date is May 2, 1987. I went into treatment on May 22, 1989, for thirty days to find out why I did things the way I did. There I found a man called Jesus Christ who became my new Higher Power. I believe that a lot of my drinking was due to pain, the way I was raised and the disappointments of life.

Jesus did not immediately solve all my problems. My drinking stopped, but all the issues that had caused my drinking were still there—the remorse for the pain I had put my family and friends through.

Even though I was no longer drinking, I was going to so many meetings that I was never home with my wife and the children. We almost separated because of that. I became very depressed and one night I found myself in a closet with a shotgun in my face. I wanted to die, and thought everything would be fine if I wasn't around. I don't know what happened, and I can't explain it—I had my toe on the trigger ready to go—but somehow I knew that Jesus had His hand on this, and I woke up the next morning, still alive, laying on the floor of the closet.

My wife and I didn't separate, and things limped along for a while and eventually began to get better as I quit going to quite as many meetings.

In September of 1992 my wife had a heart attack and she needed a heart transplant in order to live. She waited in the hospital from September 3 until December 28 of 1992. She died on the operating table. I felt she died from a broken heart. They couldn't help her. We had been married just shy of twenty-five years. My meetings increased.

Even with attending many meetings, my world was crushed. I didn't know what to do. My brother told me to move out west, so I did so that I could be closer to them. I was still carrying a load of guilt, and I had a lot of time on my hands. I had confessed all my sins, but I had never tried to make amends for many of them. I decided to go back and look up people I had offended over the years, and ask for their forgiveness. I tried to make things right and my load began to get lighter.

In 1995 I met my third wife, Sue, and we were married in 1997. I moved to Torrington, Wyoming, with her. We began going to the Henry Methodist church which we fell in love with, and started worshiping Jesus together. As we grew more in love with Jesus, we grew more in love with each other.

In 2008 we moved to Douglas, Wyoming. In September of that year we went to a church called The Gathering. We fell in love with this church! Last year I started going to Bible Study with Pastor and others. I have learned so much about Jesus and the Word of God! This last December 2009, I asked the Lord to take my life and worries into His hands and give me peace and serenity and He answered my prayer.

Today I have no worries and I am learning to trust Him in all things. On July 25, 2010, I was baptized in the LaPrele Creek at Natural Bridge.

Today above all, I love the Lord my Savior with all my heart and soul! I look to Him for everything on a daily basis, and He never lets me down. Thank You Lord!

Never An Instantaneous Event

Sue Ragland

I am a Christian. I am also a recovering alcoholic. Most of my life has been dominated by my feelings, not by facts or faith—but by feelings. Let me tell you, your feelings can really take you on a wild ride!

As far back as I can remember I had the feeling that I didn't matter to anyone. As a child I would plan out things to do to get attention—even if it was negative attention. Two incidents are especially burned in my mind.

One day my mother returned from the store, set groceries on the table, and left to see what one of the neighbor ladies wanted. There were a lot of us to feed in my family, so I figured what I was about to do would get her attention. While waiting for my mother to return I ate a whole bag of chips and an entire head of lettuce. I felt extremely guilty and lonely. I cried the whole time. I also felt scared, but no one ever mentioned this happening. It was as if I didn't exist!

The other plan I had was to smoke a cigarette. I stole it from my mother's pack and went to the bedroom. I lit it and listened for her approach. Again, I was scared, and I felt so alone! When I did hear her coming, I put the lit cigarette on the rug, under the bed and placed the ashtray over it. My mother simply removed everything from under the bed and left the room. It seemed like I was invisible—no interaction, no nothing!

In fourth grade I remember a pervading anger and sadness. My mother had made me a coat for Christmas out of the material from an old coat. The material was gray, scratchy wool. I knew she meant well, but I still was angry about something. I stood under a rain spout and soaked the coat and myself. My warm coat was ruined and no one said a word about it to me.

Through my elementary years, I was dropped off at church for Christmas and Easter. Later, I still managed to get confirmed even though I skipped out on most of the classes. Though I didn't go to my own church much, I went to Sunday school almost every week—at least when the kids at school would invite me and could pick me up. I went to almost every denomination there is. It was fun learning about Jesus and the Bible, but every time I went I felt guilty, not worthy. I felt that I wasn't good enough for Jesus to love me. I felt like a phony.

When I was around nine years old, I was outside in the yard on a beautiful summer day. I suddenly felt devastated, lonely, and heartbroken. I looked up at the cloudless, clear blue sky, and I thought *God, is this all there is?*

Today, I remember that sad, hopeless little girl and I want to hug her and tell her I love her.

In Junior High and High School I found something that could take away my pain and loneliness. I began to drink all the time and would stay out at night. My first alcoholic black-out was when I was fourteen years old. Over the next twenty-two years, I was on a mission to find the person, place or thing to make me feel good.

I got married when I was sixteen. I had two children by the time I was eighteen. My first husband beat me regularly, but I stayed in this relationship for seven years because my husband and I both thought it was 'normal.' Both of our mothers were beaten by their husbands, so it seemed that everything was the way it had always been.

But over the next twenty-five years, I went on to marry ***seven more times***. I was on the journey to find someone that would make me happy. Sadly, I believed sex was love. It felt good for a while, and each time I married I truly believed it was for life.

Before giving my life to Christ I was an alcoholic; I was promiscuous, self-absorbed, dishonest, workaholic, cold-hearted, perfectionist, judgmental and a gossip. I was materialistic and spent money I didn't have just to try to impress others with my car, house, clothes and other things. *Stuff.* I spent a good part of my time blaming others for my problems. Like a destructive tornado, I gathered people, places and things, and left wreckage in my wake and never looked back. My lifestyle led me to a DUI, a night in jail, and eventually a treatment center.

Coming to Christ has been a process for me—not an instantaneous event. In fact, it has been a process that has spanned twenty years. It began the day Jesus met me in my dining room and told me *You don't have to do it alone.* He took the desire to drink away from me that day.

After a week in treatment I learned that I was an alcoholic. I learned that it is a disease and it is treatable. Often it takes time to change and we don't accomplish it alone. I have come to believe that I am worthwhile by learning to change the way I think. For years AA was my spiritual family. Through AA I found God as my higher power. I could meet with my spiritual family anywhere in the world by just walking into an AA meeting and I would find immediate acceptance.

When I began attending Henry Church Fellowship in Nebraska it had the most profound spiritual effect on my life—in my walk with God. It was there that I realized that

Jesus loves me—that I was lovable—that I can never be good enough—but that Jesus died for *my* sins! Jesus loves me! Jesus forgives me!

Knowing Christ as my Savior has made several changes in my life. Today I am comfortable in my own skin. I possess more empathy and sympathy. I reach out more and am available to help others more. I have taken full responsibility for my own actions and decisions. I am no longer materialistic. I am trying my best to avoid and not participate in gossip or any negativity. I seek God's will for my daily life. I am able to love others unconditionally in the same way Jesus loves me.

I have finally learned to accept life on life's terms. I can trust people with my true feelings and I pray to express my gratitude to God daily. I pray for help in making decisions. I pray when I am in pain.

Gene is the love of my life. We love each other with all our scars, bumps and imperfections. We are there for each other even though we are different in many ways. We know each other inside and out and have complete trust with each other's feelings. I praise God for bringing us together, and for helping us learn new things together along the way.

Some things that I believe God is teaching me right now in my life are that I've held on to too much guilt. I've hurt many people in my life and I need to accept God's complete forgiveness in that. My adult son committed suicide three years ago, and I still wonder how I could have saved my son.

I want to be the kind of person God wants me to be so that my other son, still living, will share his life with me. The writing and speaking of this testimony has been a big thing for me. I believe God is leading me to a new phase in my life. I'm a little bit afraid and apprehensive, but also willing and excited.

Lately, as Pastor Frank talks about His Father in heaven, I've come to trust My Father in Heaven for the first time. He holds me in His arms. He consoles me and wipes away all my tears. He blesses me and laughs with me.

Finally, after all these miles and years, My Father in heaven is urging me to let Him carry my burdens and move on.

It is a pleasure to share my story of faith.

Painful Reality— Personal Relationship

Linda Carlat

I grew up in a home that was very confusing as far as spiritually. My mom was very strict and devoted to her church. She made sure that all of us knew the rules and traditions of the church. On the other hand, my dad wanted nothing to do with anything spiritual or religious, and he was especially disdainful of a ritualistic church. I would listen to both sides of their argument and didn't ever really know who was right.

At home, there was a Bible that sat up on a shelf. When I was a child and told to dust that shelf, I remember taking that Bible down and reading it.

I was never a wild and crazy kid, and all of my friends were Christians. They often tried to show me the truth, but frankly, I didn't think I needed anything because I was a 'good girl.' I didn't catch on to the truth until the Lord brought Dan into my life when I got out of high school. Dan was the man I wanted to spend the rest of my life with, but we never talked about marriage. It was like we just knew that we *would* be married. But about a month into our relationship Dan told me that he could not marry me because I was not a saved Christian. He continued to explain that the Bible says not to be unequally yoked. I had no idea what he was talking about. He took the time to tell me about it and explained it clearly to me. When I came to understand the truth, Dan and I prayed. It was then that I accepted the Lord as my Savior. I was twenty years old.

I read my Bible but not with the intention of knowing the Lord personally or finding out what He wanted from me. I did it to prove that everything that I had learned from my mother and her church was wrong. (Not exactly what God had in mind!) I continued on in what I thought was a Christian life. Dan and I had two children and when I was pregnant with our third, a doctor's visit revealed complications with the baby. We were told that either I or the baby could die, and were the baby to live, chances are it would be disfigured. Instead of going to Jesus I listened to the doctors and made a very painful decision. I chose to abort my baby, and to this day it remains a very painful reality for me.

At that time I had a wonderful friend who was an amazing Christ-follower. Her name was Nell. She loved the Lord with her whole being, and I couldn't tell this great friend about my shame in making the choice that I had made about that baby. But one day she gave me a book to read called "Tilly." The story told about a baby that was aborted and went back to heaven. After reading it, the tears came and I was able to share with Nell what I had done. Nell told me *Jesus forgives you, now forgive yourself.*

I wanted so much to be like Nell but I didn't have a clue as to how to reach that level. I continued trying to get there by my own power, and I knew that Jesus was there. I hadn't given Him my whole life, and I didn't know how to open my heart to Him. I would try and read the Bible, but the words were jumbled, and the messages didn't seem clear to me.

When I was thirty-four years old, lumps began appearing all over my body. At first, the doctors didn't know what it was, and things started to shut down. I lost control of my eye movement and I couldn't swallow. After a three-week hospital stay, I was diagnosed with stage four Hodgkin's Disease—a terminal stage of cancer. I felt very much alone, but one day while reading my Bible, the words **I WILL NOT LET YOU DIE** jumped out at me as if they were in 3D. I clung to those words and felt my heart begin to soften.

Not long after my very first chemo treatment I was healed of cancer. All the doctors could say was *We see this sometimes but we can't explain it.* But **I knew** the Lord had healed me. I continued on with eight months of chemo treatments and two weeks of radiation treatments. Why did I? Maybe it was God telling me to, or maybe it was my hesitation to believe that God could really heal me. Whatever! God healed me either because of the treatment, or in spite of it! I still know that it was God who healed me.

After the cancer, I continued to live my Christian life and continued to attempt it on my own. I was living my dream life as a rancher's wife. I had a great husband, three kids, four hundred cows and seven horses. Life was good!

But then, it all changed literally overnight. I was forty-eight years old when I woke one morning with Dan explaining to me that I had suffered a major stroke. The last thing I could remember was going to bed after carpel tunnel surgery. It was a month later and Dan struggled attempting to tell me what had happened.

There are bits and pieces of that month that seem somewhat clear, but not much. I realized that this situation was a major one, and I couldn't do anything by myself. I was unable to change positions while laying down, I couldn't watch TV and worst of all, I couldn't sit up or hold a book or magazine to read. I couldn't read my Bible. I tried to figure out how to commit suicide to be free from it all, but I couldn't even do that without help. Everything I once had, I could no longer enjoy. I felt that my life was over.

One day, Dan was taking me to physical therapy and for some reason I was alone in the car for a time. Everything seemed to weigh heavily upon me. My self-pity was suffocating me. I cried out to Jesus and finally admitted that I couldn't do it on my own . . . ***I couldn't do anything on my own!*** I needed His help. I asked Him to come into my sinful life and help me.

That day at therapy I was fitted with my first brace which helped me 'sort-of' walk. My left side didn't work but I was learning to balance which helped me to walk. Dan kept looking into different ways that would improve my condition. Later on, we heard about a treatment that had helped other stroke victims, and the Lord led us to the Hypobaric Chamber. This is a machine that is used by divers when they come up to the surface too quickly. It saturates your entire body with pure oxygen, and the use of this machine brought more oxygen to my cells and began healing me. Dan did a lot of research, and the Lord once again helped us. We managed to obtain a portable chamber for our home. I took treatments once a day for one hour, and in the chamber, with the steady hissing of the machine in the background, I began to read the Bible again.

Even though my Saviour had always been there for me, I hadn't let Him completely into my heart, or given Him my whole life. I had much more to learn.

Seven years after the stroke I got cancer again. It was the same kind as the first kind, but appeared in a different part of my body. This is very rare, and I was the exception to the rule in having the same kind of cancer twice. This time, the Lord chose not to heal me immediately. Instead, He gave me the strength to get through chemo and eventually beat the cancer.

Six months after He allowed me to be cured of the cancer, He took my best friend; my caregiver—the love of my life. Dan went home to be with Him. I find peace and rejoice in the Lord that I will see Dan again, and I rest assured that I will one day walk the streets of paradise with my best friends: Jesus, Dan and Nell. Oh, what a joyous occasion that will be!

As things are today, it is still hard. The left side of my body still does not work right, but the Lord has allowed me to do more than the doctors ever thought I would. I have the Lord and Dan to thank for that. Without either one of them I would not have made it as far as I have. I know that I can do all things through Christ who gives me strength! He also has blessed me with two wonderful sons and a wonderful daughter *plus* nine grandkids to do all the things I need help with. God taught me that it's okay to ask for help.

I now know what it was that Nell possessed and what I had wanted so badly. I didn't understand how to acquire it: the personal relationship with Jesus. But just being saved is not what it's about, it is the personal relationship with the Lord that makes all the difference! We should let Him lead us every day.

Jesus has brought me to a place where I now ask the Holy Spirit to open my eyes of understanding when I read the word. Oh, how He has come to life for me! Jesus is still working on me. There are still things I want, but I'm learning to trust Him, and I realize that He knows better than I do what is best for me. I pick up my cross daily and follow Him.

In God We Trust

Shelagh (Wisdom) Basso

Overlooking the softly rolling foothills that reach toward Laramie Peak, there is a rugged point flanked by badlands that stretch down to our lower pasture. It is here that I once found my father, sitting in his truck alone and thoughtfully pondering whatever might be heavy on his heart. I was intrigued to find him there, because it was the same place that I often wandered off to when things overwhelmed me, or when I wanted to talk to God.

My dad and I referred to the place as "the hill." The simplistic name doesn't do justice to the landmark and the magnificent view it provides, nor the peace that is found there and what the location represents for me. It is there that I sincerely began my journey to Jesus, and hungered for a closer and more intimate relationship with Him.

My religious grooming through childhood and my teens was mostly self-taught. My mother bought me a beautiful children's Bible storybook that I can remember well, and my aunt and uncle sponsored me in Job's Daughters. There, I learned verses from the Bible, the words and music to many beautiful hymns, and I learned how to pray. I came to find peace and comfort in prayer. The rituals, messages, inspiration, and knowledge gained from Job's Daughters provided a solid foundation to becoming a Christian, but I didn't understand fully what it was to really know God.

Life seemed good for me, in spite of a complicated family background which never seemed very clear. I was in my late teens, and had just won my first championship team roping buckle and an all-around runner up award. The same day I received exciting news that a horse I recently trained had qualified for the National Championship Quarter Horse Congress, and another horse I had in training was a prime contender in a world-class barrel racing futurity. I was enjoying the status of being a knowledgeable horseman, a good stockman, a talented writer, and an accomplished pianist. I felt so lucky! But what I was, was truly blessed by God.

But in spite of the great things that happened on this particular day I found out that my father—my best friend, advocate, protector, teacher, and buddy—had been diagnosed with cancer. He would be undergoing surgery to remove his larynx. He wouldn't be able to talk, and I wondered *how can I ever remember his voice, or hear about how he homesteaded in 1913, how he acquired his horses and cattle, and how he raised winter wheat?*

As was typical for me in times of trouble, I saddled my horse and rode to "the hill." It was late afternoon in mid-autumn, and the sun was warm on my face. A soft breeze blew currents of ever-changing air over me from cool to warm, then almost cold and back to warm. I closed my eyes, contemplating the riches of my life: parents, home, friends, family, abilities, experiences, and future. I considered with reverence the beauty of nature and the animals that embellish it. Still, I felt ill-equipped to deal with the possibility that I might lose my father. There was something in my heart that ached for something I could not describe. I wondered about heaven and what it might be like, and I pictured my father there, greeting his old friends and family who had gone before him. I wondered about how I could stop that empty ache in my heart.

Standing there on that point, with the sinking sun throwing golden streaks of fading light up and down the draws, lavender and copper pastels caressing clumps of blue sage with gentle, fragrant fingers, I closed my eyes and prayed, *Dear God, help me be strong, help me understand what my father needs from me, help me find comfort and peace, and help me understand what You need from me.*

I didn't need to wait long. It was as if He whispered in my ear and covered me in a soft, warm blanket that fell gently over and all around me. I knew I had opened my heart, and I asked Him to come into my heart, and accepted him as my Saviour. I told Him of my sins, and asked Him to forgive me. I had entered into His light, but I still didn't really *know* Him, as I came to realize later.

I continued to learn God's word, and lean on Him through life's trials. When my father died in 1981, I was 29 years old. I remember being with my father when he drew his last breath, and I thanked God for understanding that I needed to be with him when he passed away. I praised God that day for the time that I had been able to spend with my dad, and for helping me be strong through it all. I once again found peace and comfort in God's presence.

When I turned thirty-eight, I met and married George. He was a Texas transport, and a cancer survivor. His first encounter with cancer occurred when he was thirteen. It had left his face disfigured, but once a person had talked with him, the disfigured face was never again noticed. George was that kind of person; good, gentle, kind, hardworking and possessive of a great sense of humor. We talked often of God and the Bible, and shared readings with each other sporadically. Both of us knew that the other had a strong faith, and that we prayed on our own. We both knew that we should pray together, but setting time aside for prayer together never seemed to be a priority.

George and I both worked jobs in town and we worked hard at home. We built up the place, acquired more cattle and horses, and had a small farm flock of sheep. We taught country swing dance classes for many years. He played on the pool league. I continued with my creative writing and coached the high school rodeo team, trained outside horses, and rodeoed.

In 1991 a horse I was training fell with me, severely and permanently injuring my legs. The year afterward, while competing in a team roping, the young horse I was riding stumbled and proceeded to 'blow up.' He fell and rolled over me, and from that incident I broke my pelvis. After I healed up to some degree, I struggled to keep training horses and rodeoing, but it became increasingly difficult for me. Sometimes the pain was so great that I had to ask George to unsaddle and care for my horses while I limped back to the pickup or the house. Still, I couldn't make myself stop doing what I loved the most—working with horses.

In 1997, I had to have both of my hips totally replaced. That pretty much ended my rodeo career, as well as riding, breaking and training horses. I wondered if I was being punished for something that I had done, and often cried out to God to restore what I felt He had taken from me. Immediately after those self-pitying times, I would feel guilty and apologize to God for blaming Him on my own selfishness. It seemed agonizing to me to no longer be able to do the things I loved the most, no matter what I did to try to improve my condition and get better.

One day, in one of George's infamous and humble, nonchalant moments, he listened patiently to me and tried to help me deal with frustration and resentment. He took my hand in his and said *Shelagh, did you ever consider that God is giving you the message that He wants you to write? Maybe He's not punishing you, but wants you to write about those things you love and share them with others.*

Those words made a lot of changes in my life. I began to read more and write more. I looked to God for wisdom and peace. George and I began to read to each other from the Bible almost daily and even more as his health failed. Still, we didn't attend church until after a twenty-three hour surgery wherein a team of eight doctors removed a cancerous tumor from his brain. That was the first of three such surgeries that finally ended George's life in 2008, because new tumors would manifest themselves on different parts of his brain.

During that time, I finally came to know God as I should. Sitting exhausted in waiting rooms, sleepless nights alone and worried in a hotel room, days of sitting at George's bedside in ICU, and hours spent on the highway driving him back and forth to treatments and appointments cultivated a larger awareness of God's greatness, power, and grace. The evening that George passed away, there was absolutely no doubt or question that he had gone to be with his Father in heaven, and that God was present with us when George drew his last breath. George's blessed and bittersweet goodbye earlier that afternoon was nothing short of a miracle. Even with the pain of losing him, I was at peace knowing that George had received God's promise and was no longer suffering.

I lived the next three years knowing that God cared for me in a special way. I dedicated part of each day to praise and worship. It became a way of life, and continues today. That practice has cultivated countless rewards both small and large.

On September 18 of 2011, I was blessed once again and married a man of great faith, a decorated Vietnam combat veteran from Kentucky. Johnny experienced all the worst parts of war. Johnny's Lieutenant continually tells me how Johnny was constantly on the front lines, placing himself between danger and those that followed him. Johnny started out as a cannoneer, and one time an enemy mortar round struck the cannon, which swing around and hit the side of Johnny's face. He suffers from TBI. His face has been crushed. He was exposed to extreme amounts of agent orange. He was sent out on the most gut-wrenching, horrific missions because he would rather go himself than risk the lives of others. Daily, he looked for that bullet with his name on it. Through it all and the pain of TBI, PTSD, and agent orange, Johnny leans on the word of God and his faith to lift him up from the wounds—both seen and unseen—that impede daily living and his quality of life. His body is ravaged by war; pain and torment reflect in his eyes. Johnny is a complicated and often misunderstood individual, but he *is* an American war hero, and he is full of the Holy Spirit. I am proud of his nobility, strength, sacrifice to country, courage, and faith. God moves through him each day, and gives him strength and perseverance to battle through the survivor's guilt, flashbacks, and extreme physical and emotional pain. Johnny, even in his worst pain, looks to God for healing and forgiveness.

Coming to Christ has been a wonderful, beautiful journey for me, even with its confusing and painful lessons. My walk with God continues, and I am at peace with the knowledge that He loves me. Jesus died for my sins, He loves me and He forgives me . . . is that so hard to accept? *Perhaps that's why it's so hard—because it's so easy.*

> *"But the fruit of the Spirit is love, joy, peace,*
> *longsuffering, gentleness, goodness, faith."*
> Galatians 5:22

The Light As It Shines

Carolee Hornbuckle

Believing in God was not something hard to grasp for me. As an adolescent I often lay on the ground and watch the clouds overhead. I was in awe of how big the earth was, and yet how much bigger was God? After all, He created the universe. God was so big in my eyes I felt he was far away, much too remote to take notice of me. I felt as if I was a speck; I was like an ant on an anthill. I believed in Jesus, although I really did not understand what his death and resurrection meant. Going to church, for me, meant rituals and memorizing prayers.

When I was a teenager I went to church with a high school friend, and the pastor of this church had an altar call for those seeking to be saved. I walked up to the front and accepted Jesus as my Savior. I really expected to feel different, but I still felt the same. For another thirty years, I continued to question if I was really saved. I knew I was a sinner. I felt I was not strong enough to be good all the time.

I always felt I was on the wrong side of the fence and could never be worthy enough to be on the right side of the fence. I felt weak in everything! I was painfully shy. I managed to get involved in abusive relationships, and all three of my daughters had different fathers. I seemed to commit one sin after another. I was living in darkness, with heartaches, pain and suffering. *How could I possibly be saved?*

I found myself pregnant at the age of nineteen, and my boyfriend offered to pay for an abortion. I refused his offer, and he quickly left town. Another male friend decided to be the gallant knight and save me; he offered to marry me. I was sure I could make this marriage work. I was going to have the little house with the white picket fence. I would cook and clean for my husband while he was providing for us. I knew he drank and smoked marijuana, but I didn't realize that he was a drug addict and alcoholic. I soon discovered that he used LSD, heroin, cocaine, and anything else he could get his hands on. He also sold drugs and had a gambling problem.

Two years into this marriage, I had another child. When I went into labor he was on one of his three-day drunks, and was nowhere to be found. Eventually I decided to leave him. He took a gun and tried to kill himself by shooting himself in the stomach in front of me as I watched.

My second husband was also an alcoholic and extremely abusive. Our home was my prison cell. I feared for my life. There may not have been bars on the windows or doors, but he still kept me in a prison. Six months into the marriage he started beating me, and he continued to beat me on a weekly basis. One morning he left for work and I decided to mail some bills. While I was at the post office he came home because he said it was too muddy for him to work. I came home from the post office and he shoved me down on the ground and began kicking me with his steel-toed work boots. I never knew what would set him off into one of his rages. He kept me isolated from friends and family.

One night while I was sleeping, he came home after the bar closed and punched me because I was not awake and expecting him. My jaw was cracked and dislocated. My dream of having the "all-American family life" where we enjoy meals and watching TV together just did not happen in our home.

Family life with Husband #2 was the life of hell. I could write a book about the horrors that my children and I went through. The only time that I was allowed to play with or hold my daughters was when he was gone. As soon as he would come home, my daughters would retreat to their bedrooms for safety. I generally ate one meal a day so that my children would have enough to eat. I often had to wait until he was passed out to sneak a couple of dollars for milk or bread, because any money we had would go to his alcohol addiction. I weigh a good thirty-four pounds more now than I did then.

But, with God's help and the help from the coalition I was delivered from this situation. It was a dream come true to finally be free to watch TV, stay up late, play with my children whenever I wanted, or go to the grocery store without fear. With the food stamps I received we had plenty to eat and we felt almost like royalty. A person does not really value freedom until they have been in bondage, and then set free.

My third husband did not drink or do drugs, so I believed that this marriage was going to work. But Husband #3 and his family believed in witchcraft. He was an atheist! No one in his family wanted to work—they all entered the Canadian lottery every week calling upon the dark forces to help them pick the winning ticket! Needless to say, I found myself divorced for a third time. When I really cried out to God, my prayers would occasionally be answered. Still, I believed I was not worthy, and I was broken down, used, damaged, and without hope.

I remember two instances that opened my eyes enough to see a glimmer of light through the darkness. My present husband, Kirk (the best husband ever)! and I attended a Bible study taught by Wes Walton. Wes taught about the tree of life, and how we are grafted into this tree when we accept

Jesus as our Savior. Wes described how the grafting into a tree does not immediately produce results; that it is a slow process. As the sap from the tree of life flows into the branch that was dying, growth starts to take place. This gave me hope and I began to read the Bible.

The second enlightening experience was spending some time with a woman who was dying of cancer. I drove her to Casper for her cancer treatments, and she somehow had a peace about her. Linda had joy and was truly a 'light.' The inner light shining from this woman was greater than anything I had ever seen. She loved Jesus, she *knew* Jesus. Here she was dying of cancer, and her husband was mean and an alcoholic. How could she have joy? I wanted this light—I was *drawn* to this light. How could I have the great faith she had? I hungered for this light with all my being!

This craving drove me to God's word. In January 2009 I became serious about studying God's word. God revealed so much to me once I made the daily commitment to study the Bible! I started out with fifteen to twenty minutes of reading the Bible, and now it's an hour or two—even three. I really began to understand the full meaning of the blood covenant, the gift of grace, God's mercy, and God's great love for us. Seeking the knowledge of God is the highlight of my day. I get an adrenaline rush from reading the Bible. How crazy is that?

I have joy, peace, and I can feel God's light shining down on me. I do not have to work at being worthy; Jesus did all the work for me! The thought of what Jesus went through the days before his crucifixion—the suffering, pain, and abuse hurled at him is unbelievable! But how willingly he went to the cross and poured out his blood for us! This thought brings me to my knees. I know what it is like to be beaten, spit on, cursed at, and treated like a worthless animal. Jesus had the power to stop this abuse, yet he took it all in silence and laid down his life for us!

Through God's word, I realized I needed to be part of a church. How was I going to be able to serve God and help others by keeping myself in isolation? Living the life of a hermit was usually most comfortable for me. I am not a social person, yet God was calling me to join a community of other believers. I have attended many churches over the years, and I knew I wanted a church where I could feel I was accepted the way I am. I did not want to be looked down upon for having been married so many times or for having a different father for each of my daughters.

I found the acceptance that I was looking for at The Gathering. I found acceptance for me just the way I am. I publicly displayed my belief in Jesus Christ as my Savior in July 2010 at Natural Bridge, when Pastor Frank performed the water baptism for those wishing to step forward and show their commitment to Jesus. I am a new creature in

Christ Jesus. I do not question my salvation anymore and I know with all my heart I am saved. ***I believe!*** I no longer feel like a little ant or a speck that God does not see. I rest assured that God is not far away, and that he is with me always.

Bandage The Hurt, Heal The Sick, Find The Lost

Deb Gorsuch

Poor choices—I could be a poster child for poor choices. My story is about choices made by me and others in my life. These choices and consequences shaped my past. This story is real, sordid—and mine. But at the end, there is one choice that I made that changed my life forever.

My parents were married six months before my birth. For anyone who knows how long woman is pregnant you can figure out I was either premature or my parents conceived me out of wedlock. What I didn't know until recently was that my mother's marriage to my father was less than the fairy tale I remembered. She chose to stay with a cheating spouse, physical and verbal abuse and financial difficulties. When she had enough, her next choice was to divorce my father and raise three children on her own. It was the early

70s and I felt like I was the only person on the planet with divorced parents. My choice was to act grown up and help my mom with my little sister and brother.

Life was hard for a single woman and kids. My Aunt Donna and her kids moved in with us for a while. Aunt Donna was a crazy, hippie flower-child who didn't wear a bra, drank a lot of wine and smoked pot. She was my mom's best friend. I came home from Aunt Donna's one time, after my mom had been partying all weekend. She was drunk and I was afraid she would drive off the cliff on the switchbacks. It was cold out and we drove home with the windows rolled down so she wouldn't fall asleep. She chose to party and drive drunk. She also had a lot of boyfriends and she worked as a bartender 'to make ends meet.' Looking back I see how the choices my mom made shaped the choices I made.

During my teen years, my mom was married to a verbally abusive, alcoholic man who had a son in college. He was so cool! He came to my room to seduce me one night. Mom caught us and he never came back. The wheels were already rolling though. I'd learned that if you drank enough you became fun and pretty and the guys really liked you. I got drunk the first time in the spring of my freshman year in high school. I remember throwing up in a field and going back for more alcohol.

I lost my virginity that summer to a boy who drank and smoked pot. The event wasn't special and it wasn't comfortable. He, of course, avoided me at school after it happened.

Some of my male friends knew the sports writer at the newspaper. He was twenty-one and he liked me. It was exciting having sex with an 'older man.' He had his own place and took me out to the bars even though I was under age. Sometimes he made me do things sexually I didn't want to do, but most of the time he was really sweet to me.

My mom said she didn't know I was having sex when she sat me down one day to see if I wanted to get on birth control. It was too late. I was sixteen and pregnant. To make matters worse he was a 'dirty Mexican.' Mom was 'too young to be a grandmother' and I had 'too much going for me.' A baby just wasn't in the picture. I told my boyfriend that Mom wanted me to have an abortion. Even though he was Catholic he went along with it and paid for the abortion.

I chose to murder my unborn child and our relationship was done.

I met some other people and eventually hooked up with someone that was supposed to be a nice boy from a good family. He was at my side and supported me through the death of my sister, and agreed to move to Cheyenne with me because we needed a new start. Eventually we married and had two beautiful boys. Later I found out my husband came from an abusive family. I was following in my mother's footsteps right down to the cheating, the emotional and verbal abuse, the financial difficulties. I lived what I learned and chose divorce.

While my husband and I were separated he told me I was old and fat and nobody was ever going to love me. I decided to prove him wrong. I got a second job bartending, started partying again and I slept with all kinds of men to prove that I wasn't unlovable. Because of my choices my ex-husband got custody of our children. I was scared, alone, broke and out to prove him wrong. I wanted to prove to him (and myself) that I wasn't old and fat, and someday somebody would love me again.

For the next fifteen years I searched for the perfect man who would love me. I slept with many men. Most of them were one-night stands but sometimes I'd find someone who would stick around for a while—until I got tired of him or he found someone else. Some of my conquests were married men. I justified it by thinking that since I wasn't married, I wasn't committing adultery. He was. Drinking, sleeping around, working two jobs, losing myself in volunteer projects—being all I could be—I was a mess. Any respect I might have had for myself was gone.

In desperation one night, I found myself drunk and alone in my house with another failed relationship breaking my heart. I cried out to someone—anyone—*Why won't someone love me, what's wrong with me?* Between sobs I heard a calm, gentle voice tell me *I love you my child.* I finally slept.

I still had lessons to learn, but I had finally met the One who truly loves me.

It would be nice to wrap up my story here and say that everything came out just peachy. It didn't. I knew then that my life was on the wrong track, but I didn't care enough or know enough to change my life. One night when I was drunk, I chose to get in a vehicle and drive drunk because I was less drunk than the friend I was driving home. I got pulled over and landed in the back seat of a cop car, hand-cuffed and pleading my story that I was just helping out a friend. Jail that night was humiliating. Breakfast the next morning convinced me I never wanted to go back there.

The judge sentenced me to alcohol education. Divine coincidence led me to a Christian counselor. During our sessions she would talk to me about going to church. I figured I didn't have anything to lose and I had a friend that was attending church at a The Gathering. I'd heard about 'that Church' and figured I could check it out. It was pretty good!

I'd been coming to The Gathering for about a month and starting to learn a little bit about this Jesus person. Sure, I believed, but I didn't get it. I thought the words to "Amazing Grace" were just words. One Sunday Pastor Frank was talking about how God loves everybody. He told us that God didn't make junk. Over and over during his message those words kept washing over me. Cleansing me. My eyes were opened by the Holy Spirit and ***I finally got it!*** God loves me. He ***really loves me!*** With the power of that understanding I started crying in disbelief and gratitude. I felt so humbled by His love and His grace! I made the greatest choice of my life and accepted Christ into my life.

Of course, right then the evil one started in with all his accusations. *What about the baby you aborted when you were sixteen? What about two failed marriages? What about the drunken nights? What about sleeping around to find acceptance? What about your ugly past? What about, what about, what about?*

STOP!

Once I accepted the forgiveness and love of God, I was able to start forgiving and accepting myself. My favorite verse in the Bible became Isaiah 1:18, "Come now, let's talk this over," says the Lord. "Though your sins are like scarlet, they shall be white as snow; though they are red as crimson, they shall be like wool."

I am forgiven.

As I started to work on my alcohol addiction, I learned how my past had shaped my life. Wrapping my mind around the enormity of God's forgiveness helped me learn that I needed to repent and take responsibility for my actions. I needed to tell people that I was sorry for things I had done. Choosing to say *"sorry,"* and really meaning it, is very liberating. I also had people I needed to forgive for past hurts done to me.

God's word in 2 Corinthians 5:17 says it best for me: "When someone becomes a Christian he becomes a brand new person inside. He is not the same any more. A new life has begun!"

I cling to God's promise that a new life has begun. I'm learning how to be a better person, more Christ-like. I know some days I don't make it—not even close—but I believe that God is directing me now through His Holy Spirit. Pastor Frank tells us we're all 'in process' and that is another truth I hold on to. I don't have to be perfect. God keeps giving me tools and teachers to learn more about His love for me . . . His love for all his children.

Ezekiel 34:16 says, "I will look for those that are lost, I bring back those that wander off, bandage those that are hurt, and heal those that are sick."

That's my choice now, too, to look for those who are lost, and to show them the love and forgiveness of Christ. To help them find peace. I have found the One who loves me like I am supposed to be loved. Actually, He was there all the time. Jesus loved me enough to die for me and because of that choice I am forgiven for the sins of my past and I have hope for my future.

God loves you that much too. He's just waiting for you to open your heart. Choose forgiveness and hope.

Fully Forgiven, Fully Forgiving

Ginger Baumann

I grew up in a family where God was a silent subject and we rarely attended church. On my eighth birthday, my grandmother gave me a pocket size New Testament. I would go through it and read all the verses she had underlined in red ink. I often read it and wondered *is this real? Is there a God out there who loves me? A Jesus who died for my sins?*

In my freshman year of high school, my best friend by the name of Maria, introduced me to God. Maria had such faith and I wished with all my heart to know for sure that God was *real.* During a sleep-over at her house in the sanctuary of her room, I expressed my doubts of the reality of God. Then as we talked, I suddenly felt the presence of God. Since that night I have never doubted God's existence. I began attending church, in fact several different kinds, searching for one where I could begin to understand God's word.

My father moved our family from place to place. We were like gypsies and I wondered if we really *were* gypsies. I remember moving eight times between six different states. From the third grade to my freshman year of high school, I took God and Jesus with me wherever we moved though the small New Testament given to me. The last move I made with my family was to Douglas, Wyoming. I graduated here and married my first husband. Then the gypsy came out in Dad again, and he moved the rest of the family to Oklahoma.

My first husband seemed like a good man . . . until after the wedding. Then I got to see the other side of him: a verbally abusive, controlling man. I confided my unhappiness to my mother. She told me that the first three to five years of marriage were the hardest, and advised me that I should endure the hard times and hope for change in the future.

God soon blessed me with a daughter. I started attending church with my father-in-law and mother-in-law. I was happy. I could see and feel the love of God, and I was gaining more in-depth knowledge of God through the services and classes I attended.

Then the church taught on baptism and I wanted to be baptized to start a fresh new walk with God at my side. I told my husband of my plans and he became very angry. He forbade me to be baptized, and he told me that if I did not obey, he would put me and our daughter out on the street with nothing. The message was loud and clear: he was to be in control, not God! This was a very unpleasant scene and the thought of being out on the street with a baby in the winter without any family nearby to turn to for help stopped all thoughts of baptism.

He chose my friends, activities, and even a different church for me to attend if I still wished to go. I think he presumed I would give up attending church, but I did not, for I wanted and needed God in my life. I started attending the church he chose, for in my heart, I knew God is not confined to just one church. I also had learned that life was easier if you did not rock the boat.

Life soon revolved around caring for the children God had blessed me with: a daughter and two sons. I did my best to be the perfect mother and wife for ten years. I became active in the church, taught Sunday school, vacation Bible school, and helped out with the women's fellowship pie project. Reading the word of God often was comforting, but still, I was not happy. Kind words were few and far between and my self-esteem was quite low. As the children grew, my husband would bribe them to stay home from church or request that they stay home. It became a tug-of-war game in order to get the children to church.

Soon I realized that you can't make someone love God or make someone kind and loving toward yourself. I started praying to God asking him to help me love my husband. I thought if I loved my husband well enough God could change him. For eight years I prayed and did my best to create a loving home for the children and my husband.

God has blessed us all with the freedom of choice. He does not force his will or what another person may will onto you. God gave me the strength to endure, but I started noticing my frustration and hurt was flowing over to the children. I was becoming what I feared most: a bitter, unhappy, hurting and negative person. I tried hard to win the love of my husband, but his main objective was control.

Realizing that I was changing, I began to doubt my faith. I loved my children very much, and I did not want them to go through or live in a divorce situation. So I set myself a new goal; to hold the marriage together until the kids graduated high school. I built a wall around myself so he could not hurt me, then a mask to cover up my sadness and give the world the illusion of a good marriage. My true friends saw through this. Realizing that my mask of happiness had failed, no longer fooling my friends or even at times myself, I desperately started looking for a way out. God seemed so far away!

A divorce would hurt the children too much and I had read in the Bible that divorce was not what God wished for his children. Suicide . . . there wouldn't be a divorce that would hurt the children, no admitting to being a failure, and the end to the hurting. The planning began—I had it all figured out—the 'when' and 'how' to end all my problems.

The day arrived—a hurting day—a day I hit bottom. I climbed into the car en route to a cliff embankment, thinking I would drive the car—with me in it—at enough speed to sail off the cliff embankment, putting an end to the years of hurting. God seemed so far, far, away. I had lost faith in Him and it seemed as if He had abandoned me. I was so tired of hurting!

As I was driving along with tears running down my face, God's voice spoke to my heart, telling me that suicide was not the answer and that suicide was a sin against Him. He told me that the marriage was not worth my life. I pulled the car over and sobbed for a long time. I returned home knowing that with all of the anguish it would entail, a divorce would be best for me and for the children. I would have to do it.

Divorce is hard for everyone. Emotions are high, and the heart is tender. I was upset with God for not fixing my problems. I managed to weather the divorce but was still searching for love. I was like a child just learning to walk and repeatedly falling down. I discovered that I was the one who had to rise up in the midst of all the pain and learn to walk with Him. God's love was always there, but at that time I just could not see it. As it is said *"It is always darkest before the dawn."* God was guiding and helping me to grow and learn about real love: His love.

I began asking God to bring a good man into my life. He blessed me with my husband, Rooster. I have often heard people talk about soul mates! God brought us together, and together we complete each other. I am so thankful and blessed! Rooster loved and nurtured me though three heart-breaking years. Together Rooster and I have blended together a new family. We have an abundance of love flowing in our new family.

About three years ago, God started working with me on forgiveness. I still had a lot of 'un-forgiveness' toward my ex-husband. God kept steering my Bible readings toward forgiveness. So I told God *I forgive, but I can't forget.*

If you say you forgive, but can't forget, have you really given forgiveness? God kept working with me and bringing up scenes of hurt from my first marriage in my mind. Slowly, with each past hurt God showed me, I would pray asking for His help and confess forgiveness. Though the grace of God, I am at peace now and have fully forgiven my first husband. I am free and I no longer recall the pain or hurt I experienced in my first marriage.

When I think back on my life now, I would not change anything. I needed all the trials in my life to grow and bring me to where I am now. I have learned that the words we speak have such power! They can encourage, build up, and love; or dishearten, tear down and cut deeper than any sword. We need to forgive in order to fully experience God's blessings of peace. Jesus said *"I come so that your joy may be full"*. Today, as a child of God, saved through the blood of Jesus Christ, and growing daily in my walk of faith, I look for ways to let God's love and blessings flow through me and extend to be a blessing to others.

To top off this joy, on July 25 of 2011, both Rooster and I were baptized in the river at Natural Bridge. It is such joy to attend church together and share our faith with each other!

Just Show Up

Pat Baumann

As a child, I was fortunate to have parents that loved me. They gave me opportunities to grow and explore. Dad and Mom wanted me to be exposed to all good things in life and religion was no exception. After I was baptized, they made sure that on most Sundays we were sitting in church. We also attended church-related events during the week and I was a member of our church's confirmation class. At that time, I didn't realize how important all of these things would be to me later in life.

When Jesus talked about the seeds that were cast upon rocks not growing, I think he was talking about me. You see, my parent's spiritual training went right out the window as soon as I left our ranch for college. I found it to be much more fun to attend beer busts and see how much I could drink than to attend church and join the congregation. In fact, my church attendance eventually dropped to nothing and my relationship with God went the same direction.

I went to church only once in those days, and that was to get married. Of course, that ceremony was preceded and followed by big parties. Big parties and drinking remained the focus of my life for many years. People used to tell me that I was the life of the party and they always told me that they liked my sense of humor. I had another side though, and my family knew it. I was seldom home on time and they couldn't count on me to keep my promises. It seemed that something would always take me away from the tasks of being a good husband and father. After years of this behavior, I found myself divorced and living alone.

Living alone had many benefits—one of them being extra time to party! I discovered, what I thought at the time, was 'better living through chemistry'. Drugs were easy to find in the crowd that I hung out with. My outlook on life soon grew just as disorderly as my long hair and my beard. At one party, I met a guy that asked me to be his business partner. Buying drugs cheap and selling them at a profit sounded pretty simple, so I took him up on his offer. We weren't much more than two-bit hoods, but we made enough money to pay for a few parties and I *did* meet a lot of colorful characters. However, I was most comfortable with those characters if I had a pistol nearby. So, I always kept one under my pillow and one in my truck . . . just in case.

One day, a biker customer of ours complained that we had cheated him. We felt that he was wrong, and we told him in no uncertain terms that he would have to go elsewhere next time. We thought that was the end of that matter. Nothing could have been further from the truth.

One night I awoke to someone pounding on my front door. When I answered it, I was startled to find a police officer standing there with the lights from his squad car flashing. He informed me that my business partner had been found in the city dump. A bullet wound to the head had killed him instantly. By that point in my life, my sensitive nature and my humor had turned sour. Although the officer was concerned for my safety, I told him matter-of-factly, that I could take care of myself. From that day forward, I carried a pistol everywhere and I constantly looked behind me and around corners for danger. After all, I could have been on the biker's list also. Eventually, the biker was locked in jail with a life sentence. That fact didn't make me feel much better and my outlook on life grew darker.

There were lies, cheating, and greed. I dreaded waking up each morning because of the insanity that each day would bring. It had become unbearable. Few people understand the feeling of total darkness that a person lives in before they consider taking their own life. It is a hopeless feeling that all is lost—a feeling of complete and total despair, with no place to turn for support. It was at that point when I put the pistol to my head. Before pulling the trigger, a strange feeling of calmness came over me. At last, I wouldn't have to live with the guilt or pain anymore. It would all be over. I still recall the sound of the hammer falling on an empty chamber and the vibration of the muzzle against my temple. Apparently God had intervened—I had forgotten to reload the chamber after an afternoon of shooting at empty beer cans. I fell on the floor into the fetal position and I cried for hours. It was a sort of nervous breakdown, I suppose, and I stayed at home for days just staring at the walls and saying *God help me . . . God please help me!*

In an attempt to start over, I invited my parents and my last remaining friend over for dinner. I sensed that they were reluctant, but they all showed up for dinner as planned. My friend made a poor remark shortly after he arrived and I punched him in the mouth. My parents helped him off the floor and gave me a look that said *where did we go wrong?* He left without dinner. My parents stayed with me as I made the decision to call a self-help hot line. As I reached out, God gave me His hand. It was at that very moment that I was reborn. The 'rock' had finally turned into a fertile field. God talked through the people on the other end of the phone and He persuaded me to join Alcoholics Anonymous. Over the years, God's seed **did** grow and through AA, I got back on my feet. I had a relationship with God again, even better than before. I explored numerous ways to worship, but I stayed with the roots of my childhood . . . Christianity.

Ironically, part of my recovery included hosting AA meetings at two state prisons and several county jails. For six years, I was a regular visitor at the very institutions that I should have been sentenced to.

It all seems so long ago. I have been sober and clean for twenty-three years now. I've shaved off my beard and cut off my pony tail. But the real changes have taken place inside. To the best of my ability, I've made amends to those that I had harmed. Now, people trust me to keep my promises and I show up on time. My greatest joys in life stem from being a husband, a father, a grandfather and a friend. I have a wonderful wife and soul mate. Last summer, we celebrated our faith by being baptized by Pastor Frank at Natural Bridge. We are grateful members of The Gathering, where we worship without denomination. We have five wonderful children and nine grandchildren. They are all precious and we are very proud of them. Our friends are truly *friends* and we can count on them through thick or thin.

Oh, by the way, I haven't found it necessary to punch any of them!

God has saved my life on at least eight occasions including several serious car wrecks. Before my ninth life ends, I hope to be a good example to my children and grandchildren as to how life should be lived. I ask God each day to let His words come from my mouth and His actions to come through my hands. Then, I go out and do my best at whatever He puts in front of me. I trust Him to guide me and I know that He has the plan. All that I have to do is show up. Each day is a new adventure and I find myself excited to do things that I didn't even know that I wanted to do!

Close Encounters Of The Godly Kind

Pat Bledsoe

As long as I can remember I've loved pandas. I read about them, looked at pictures and saw cartoons about them. They were fascinating and I thought of them as mystical or mythological creatures.

The first time I actually saw a panda I was at the Natioinal Zoo in Washington, DC. I stood amazed and stared in wonder. No longer were these animals one-dimensional. As I observed them, they observed me. I left with an even deeper appreciation of pandas.

My Christian growth has been very much like my experience with pandas. I grew up going to church every Sunday. There was never any doubt that God existed and Jesus was his son. I read the Bible and saw drawings of Biblical events. I knew it was true because my mother told me it was.

I was baptized when I was sixteen because that was the time when most of my friends were baptized. I believed in Jesus so that's what I was supposed to do. I was in the church youth choir and traveled to different states singing a rock musical called "Natural High." I went to church every Sunday, Sunday night, and Wednesday.

I sang about God, I prayed, and I read, but something was still missing. I remember on one of my choir trips I went into an empty church in Wisconsin and begged God to give me a sign that He was there. There was only silence.

I spent the next thirty-five years searching off and on for God. I knew He was there, but I had no idea how to relate to Him. My mother was close to God but she died when I was twenty-three, before I could ask her what her secret was. I assumed God looked down on her with favor because she was such a good person. I, on the other hand was unworthy of anyone's love.

I made a conscious decision to have fun until I was thirty and then be 'good.' I had already decided that I was a failure so I may as well have fun for a while before once again attempting to be good. I stuck to my plan and quit smoking, drinking, and other harmful things by the time I was thirty.

I started looking for a church. At first I experimented with one every few months. Then the urge became stronger. I needed to find a connection with God. In my mid-thirties, I finally found a church. It was an Episcopal Church, which was totally different from the way I was raised, but a good friend went there and she drove me every Sunday. I was in the process of losing my vision and could no longer drive, so going with her was like a gift from God.

I started to feel that God was working in my life. Little coincidences happened, liked going for a walk and having my Walkman radio pick up only Christian stations. I started to feel an excitement I had never felt before. Then tragedy struck.

My friend was hit by someone that ran a stop sign. Her eleven-year-old son was with her. A split second before they were hit, he spoke his last words: "Mom, I'm just going to take my seat belt off for a minute."

He was thrown out of the vehicle and died on the scene, at the edge of his property and mere seconds away from arriving safely home.

His death could only have occurred if the timing was exact. He had to be at a remote intersection at the exact moment someone ran the stop sign and he had to have just unbuckled his seat belt. My faith was shaken. I didn't blame God for the accident, but at the same time I couldn't understand why such faithful Christians had to suffer in a way that hinged on such incredibly precise and horrific timing.

My husband said, "God doesn't hurt people, but he doesn't help people either. He stays completely out of our lives." For some unknown reason, I believed him. I gathered all my religious books except for a couple of Bibles and donated them to a nearby church. Maybe I imagined that I had been getting close to God. The joy I had started to feel was replaced with emptiness.

Years passed. I still believed in God, and occasionally something would happen that I thought He had done, but my husband's words haunted me.

My grandmother died in 2001. She had told her children and grandchildren many years before her death that she wanted her personal testimony read at her funeral. When I discovered no one planned on fulfilling her request, I demanded that it be done. My relatives unanimously decided that if it was to be done, I would have to do it.

I rewrote her words so they would be large enough for me to read at the service. Then I practiced them all the way to the chapel. I was practically shaking when it was time for me to speak to the crowd of people that came to say goodbye to my grandmother.

I had difficulty walking up to the podium because I was still recuperating from a near fatal car accident. I looked down at my paper and it was too dark for me to see what was written. I started to panic.

A cloud moved, uncovering the sun, and suddenly light came in through a window behind me and landed on my grandmother's words. I was able to fulfill her request. I knew God had been there that day, but I felt He was there because of my grandmother, not because of me. Nevertheless, I was thankful for His help.

When I came to Wyoming after the failure of a twenty-five year marriage, God really started working on me. I saw an article about The Gathering in the newspaper and it created the desire to resume my search.

I was in an abusive relationship and I needed a safe place. I attended The Gathering Place, sat in the back on a couch and cried during Pastor Frank's sermons. One day, a friend said some words to me to encourage me to get out of my unhealthy relationship. She used an analogy I had never heard before. When I finally mustered the courage to talk to Pastor Frank about it, he used the same words to encourage me. I knew God was speaking to me.

Suddenly, my life made sense. I could see how God had been talking to me all along. I could see how I had ignored Him. I could identify precise moments when He had told me to go one way and I had chosen to go another. God insisted on talking to me, still trying to get my attention.

Since that moment, I have been growing in Christ and I see God working constantly in my life. I never felt important enough for God to want to have a personal relationship with me. It never occurred to me that it could happen.

He led me to find my house before it was on the market. My house is close to church and has crosswalks on each street I have to cross to get there.

He led me to put my trust in Him, quit my job, and go back to college. Immediately, I started receiving unexpected refunds and checks—enough to sustain me until I graduate.

Speaking in front of people is one of my greatest fears, but God told me to lead a Bible study. I felt Him strongly urging me to do the study and I obeyed. Then He told me to provide the books free of charge. I didn't even have a job, but I had learned my lesson. *Never ignore God.* I ordered the books. The next day, I received a check in the mail covering the costs!

God is with me always. I feel His presence and I listen to what he tells me. God remains persistent and patient, and he never gives up on me. Sometimes, knowing I can be slow to recognize his whispers, God puts things directly in front of my face and repeats His request, making it impossible for me to miss. I've been very stubborn and God has continued to break down my pride and show me His love. I am no longer alone.

What I learned about the pandas is similar to what I learned about God. God existed but He seemed untouchable, too amazing to exist in a space where I could know Him. I needed a close encounter with Him to learn that He is as real and as close as the air I breathe. He has given me that experience. My awe and wonder have been restored and I see God as He is—my personal savior, not an unreachable, mystic being.

Be Still And Know

Susan Foley

I grew up knowing all about Jesus—or so I thought. I was fortunate to have been raised in a house where we went to church faithfully every Sunday . . . or else. We did not read the Bible or pray except for the occasional rote prayer before a meal. Faith was a very private matter and not really appropriate for public discussion except within the confines of the church. But still, I am grateful for what I learned because as I matured, I knew where to turn whenever I became aware of the unmanageability of my life.

Through the fault of no one in particular, I had no self-esteem as a child. I was smart enough that I could do well in school without having to try very hard. But little girls want to be beautiful, not smart. And I was not beautiful. I was frequently mistaken for a boy. I was introverted and shy. Early in my teen years I discovered a way to make sure that I was 'liked' by the boys and never realized that I was growing into a young woman who was actually attractive.

It didn't help that I suffered from major depression. Out of desperation and some nudging from a God who really loved me, I began reading my giant, heavy, coffee-table-sized Bible. It brought me a lot of comfort, but not much understanding. I began to pray. They were the self-centered prayers of a lost and broken teenager, but they were heard and honored by God.

I survived a time when I believed that taking my own life was a reasonable option. Two times I tried to kill myself, only to have God say "NO." I believed that I was unlovable and that even God himself would soon tire of me, just as my extensive list of boyfriends had. But God never did.

Even through the five years that I spent in a band, playing the LA club circuit and living the life of "sex, drugs, and rock-n-roll," He stood by me and protected me. There is no other explanation for me having survived those years without dying of an overdose, getting killed while driving drunk or high, or getting AIDS or becoming one of the many "Female Body Found on Mullholland Drive" headlines. I hated myself and believed that I was worse than a prostitute. At least they got paid in cash. My payment was a momentary fantasy that I was loved. I didn't fear death in those days. What I feared was life, so I lived on the edge.

I can look back now and see God's constant intervention, but I was a long way from turning my life over to him. He was a constant that I would turn to only when I was desperate. I did a lot of surviving in those days, but very little living. You see, I didn't have an accurate understanding of God. I believed that He loved me as earthly people loved me. I knew how badly I had messed up in my life so I was filled with shame and guilt. I felt condemned by God, not forgiven. He was an entity that coolly floated above the mortals, watching and taking note of every failure and weakness.

I could easily see Him in my mind's eye shaking his head in disappointment over my many flaws as he added yet another check mark to the 'failures' column on my heavenly report card. My imaginary list of failures outweighed my imaginary list of holy moments so I felt no real hope of salvation. Deep inside I knew that there was something wrong with my perception of God. It didn't jive with Jesus and his actions, or the things he said. But I knew what I had been taught, and I had been taught that I was going to have to pay . . . big time.

At the age of twenty-seven I found myself with a long string of unsuccessful relationships behind me. By this time, I was a nurse. I had gone to nursing school so I could make enough money to support my music career. I gave up on finding a soul mate, and decided I would throw myself back into school to be a doctor. I swore off romance, and made the conscious decision to not date anyone seriously until after I graduated. Naturally, that's when I met my husband. We were married five months later.

My husband and I began attending non-denominational churches. I soon realized that I had a religion but not a relationship with God. I believed all of the right things, but I missed the most important things that God had to say, such as *I made you, I love you, I forgive you, and I want you to know me.* Even though I had been baptized as an infant, I elected to be baptized again. This was the start of a slow, amazing journey.

Michael and I had been married for nine months when he was car-jacked and beaten near downtown Denver. Shortly after that, I went to see a counselor and, during my first session, she somehow opened a vault of memories that brought back every pain and sorrow that had shaped my life. Things that I knew but rarely thought about suddenly hit me like a bucket of cold water. I never went back.

I got a few books to try to read in the attempt to 'self-help' myself. What a waste of time and money! I was filled with anger and resentment, self-loathing, guilt, and bitterness. And I found out that a broken person cannot fix themselves.

Over the next several years, my relationship with Jesus continued to grow, but I was still afraid of becoming one of 'those' Christians. You know the kind I mean—the ones that are pleasant all the time, even when people say cruel things about them. They listen to nothing but Christian music and watch only wholesome films. They say uncomfortable things like *God bless you* and *Praise God*. They just don't fit in with the world around them. All I ever wanted was to fit in with the world around me.

The thought of changing into 'one of those' terrified me. I didn't want people to feel about me the way I felt about 'those' Christians. They made me uncomfortable. I much preferred being the life of the party. I could drink with the best. I always had a joke or snappy come-back that was usually very crude and inappropriate. My vocabulary was riddled with expletives.

I was growing. But I was very reluctant to let God change me.

In my mid-thirties, I finally asked my doctor about my failure to get pregnant. It was discovered that I had a very small tumor on my pituitary gland that prevents my getting pregnant. I was more devastated then I would ever let anyone know. All I had ever visualized for my life was being a wife and mother. I was sure that I was being punished for my early promiscuity and immorality.

All of our closest friends were having babies. Every birthday party and baby shower was agonizing for me. I would cry all the way home, trying hard not to let Michael see. We were pressured by family, friends, and doctors to see fertility specialists and explore our options. But, in spite of the pain, we both had peace in our hearts that God knew our desires and had something in mind for us.

We discussed being full-time missionaries and other things that God might be calling us to. During this time, I clung to the scripture "Be still and know that I am God." I have always loosely translated this in my mind to *shut up, sit down, and let me do my job.* And we did. He delivered two remarkable children to us through adoption without our having to do a thing to find them.

During this time in our life, we developed an amazing support system and our faith really started to take off. We became very involved in the church and it was the best period of my life to that point. Throughout a time when our lives were full of stress and uncertainty and emotional upheaval, we found peace in the arms of God.

The 'old me' began to break away, and a 'new me' began to emerge. We made great new friends and yet I didn't lose the old friends like I thought I would. In fact, my old friends began to treat me with more respect and to seek my counsel when things went wrong in their life. People that I thought would reject me as my faith grew would come to me and ask me to pray for them when trouble came their way. And God was able to use a big 'loser'—like me—to bless others.

God continues to work in me. Yes, I have become one of 'those' Christians! I love Christian music and movies and books. I have become active in missions work, especially medical missions to Africa where I have been privileged to go three times.

I have many friends who are uncomfortable with my faith, but I won't hide it from them. I am learning to praise God in the bad times as well as the good, and to wait faithfully to see what remarkable things He is going to do through life's trials and tribulations.

I know that I have a long way to go before He will be done with me, but I can't deny his faithfulness and love for me. I can't understand it, but I could never deny it. I'm in love with my Savior and I don't care who knows it. I am no longer that teenager who feared nothing more than human rejection. I am a daughter of the King and I have a purpose here on earth. I am worth as much to the Creator of the universe as anything else he has ever created. How's that for self-esteem? I have become a new creation in Christ and for that I say unashamedly ***Praise God!***

Let Go, Let God

Sharon Jensen

When I was growing up we went to church only on the holidays. I did go to what they called Tuesday school at the church we attended but really never listened to what was being said. It was more a social time for me. Once I hit my teens years I started searching for something, but I'm here to tell you that it wasn't God. I don't know exactly what it was, but it ended up involving guys and booze.

I grew up on a ranch and for the most part my life was pretty good. My dad had a wicked temper, and was verbally abusive. At times he was physically abusive to my mom. It wasn't until much later I found out how much that affected me.

During my teen and young adult years I was pretty wild. I'm thankful that even then God had his hand on me. I didn't contract some deadly disease or kill myself while driving drunk.

I met my first husband in a bar. After we got married I wanted to have a baby right away and we did. That marriage didn't last long and I moved back to my home town with my young son.

My sister and brother-in-law were active in their church and I started hanging out with them. I accepted Christ as my Savior on Easter Sunday in 1986. I met Monty a couple months after that and we were married in January of 1987. When we first met I told him that God was #1 and my son was #2 in my life and if he wanted to be involved with me he had to know these things right off. Monty was willing to go to church and different functions with me and he got saved at a Lowell Lundstrom crusade in October of 1986.

We tried to follow God, but often times we followed our own version of what we thought was right. We dated, if that is what you want to call it, for only six months before we got married and I wasn't even divorced until right before we got married. I was pretty sure I was still in love with my first husband but I thought for whatever reason that I needed a man in my life and I wanted to move on.

I got pregnant with our daughter a month after we got married. Things were a little rough for us. I was very much in control of everything in our life as the result of watching my dad beat and belittle my mother. It wasn't going to happen to me! I remember telling Monty *take me like I am or leave*. I wasn't about to change.

Monty was younger than I and had demons of his own that he was dealing with. For the most part he did or went along with everything I said. I ran our household lock, stock and barrel. When he tried to take the authority after we had heard a message at church that men were supposed to be the head of their household all hell would break loose in our house. I had—as much as I hated it—my dad's temper. And I had (and actually still have) a pretty sharp tongue. I could cut him or anyone that dared to question me down to nothing with it.

Although we were going to church and learning the way to follow Christ and living a healthy married life, there was always something just not right. Many times throughout our marriage I threatened to leave. I would tell Monty how unhappy I was and tell him what I wanted him to do to make me happy. Remember we were 'practicing Christians.' We were very involved in our church. There were few times that Monty would say he couldn't take it anymore and wanted out of the marriage, but I would convince him or bully him in to staying.

Time moved along and Monty got his 'dream job.' He became a city police officer in the small town we lived in. The job turned into a nightmare. Being a small town, if you don't do things the way people think you should, they start rumors. And boy, did the rumors fly about Monty! It was very hard on us. At the same time, our church seemed to turn on us. We had been very, very involved with it for thirteen years! They were not there to support us during a difficult time. As a matter of fact, they pretty much threw us under the bus. I decided that I didn't want anything to do with it anymore. The old cliché of *"If this is what Christianity is I don't want anything to do with it"* fit my theory perfectly.

I led my family out of church and away from God. Monty, being who he was, didn't and probably couldn't have stopped me. I threw away all my Christian music and movies. **Everything!** We stopped going to church. At one point I started thinking that all this Christianity stuff was just propaganda. The period of living with a bad attitude lasted for around seven years. **Seven years with no God!** It is one of my biggest regrets in life. My kids were entering their teen years—a time when they needed God and a church family. I single-handedly led them away from both.

Monty changed jobs when our daughter graduated from high school and we moved from this very small, vicious town. A lot of our Christian friends were getting divorced and I remember asking Monty *This won't happen to us, right?* He assured me that it wouldn't. It wasn't but five months later and it **was** happening to us.

We had just celebrated Thanksgiving with our kids. Monty had been acting 'weird.' I don't know where it came from, but I asked him "Are you going to divorce me?" It was a random question, but his answer would change my life forever. He said "Well I was going to wait until after Christmas, but yes, I want a divorce." I was in shock to say the least. There was no talking to him. He had reached the point of no return.

That night, after over seven years, I cried out to God. I didn't know where else to turn as my world was being torn apart. And true to who He is, God was right there. I heard Him say to me as if He was sitting in the room with me, *Welcome back, I have been waiting for you.* I also heard Him say that Monty and I would be married for a very long time and what I was about to go through would be used for the glory of God.

Up until the time we left the church I thought that I was a good Christian. I thought I walked the walk and talked the talk. I read my Bible and did my best to follow God. My true walk with God did not begin until one autumn day in November. Monty and I had been married almost twenty years and he decided he'd had enough.

I moved out of our house and this started the most amazing time of awakening and renewal in my life. God was so close to me through this whole time! He walked right by my side and spoke to my heart often. God kept me going. I read books and started therapy, all the time hanging on to the promise from God that I heard that night that Monty and I would be married for a very long time. People would tell me I needed a lawyer and I said "No. I'm not getting a divorce."

Montana is a 'no contest' state, meaning if one spouse wants a divorce there really isn't anything the other can do to stop it. But I knew that God was on my side and if anyone could stop this divorce it would be Him.

In short order, God started revealing a whole lot about me to me that wasn't very pleasing. I didn't blame Monty for wanting out. God and I had some pretty heavy-duty sessions and for the first time in my life I saw myself for who I was: a controlling, over-bearing, and very selfish woman. I learned that most of this behavior probably stemmed from my childhood. I didn't want to be my mother. I had watched her be beaten, put down and then abandoned by my dad after twenty-five years of marriage. I determined early on that if I controlled everything this kind of stuff would never happen to me.

But here I was, right where I didn't ever want to be. I found that I had put a wall up around my heart, and to protect myself I tried to control everything, including God. I figured out that I had never had peace in my life because I never would let down my guard. During this time of turmoil I found real peace for the first time, and it changed my life forever.

I told Monty he could divorce me if he wanted to, but I knew that we would be back together. I told him it didn't matter to me what he did, I still loved him and knew that God had a plan for us. Monty didn't want to hear anything

I had to say and continued on with his quest for a divorce. My husband of twenty years had turned into someone that I didn't know.

I had at last started my journey to being who God intended me to be. I had found peace and I realized I didn't need to control, but instead, **trust** in God. I remember someone saying to me that my daughter was just like me, and I thought *oh no, my poor baby!* But God spoke to my heart telling me that He created me and my daughter just the way we were and He loved us. It was huge to me to know that He loved me just the way I was . . . with a few changes.

I wanted to show Monty the **new** me. In one of the books that I had read it said I needed to spend as much time with Monty as he would allow. He was doing everything he could to stay away from me. For the first time in our married life I was not in control of our marriage. But I knew who was, and boy! Was I glad that the Creator of the Universe was in control of my marriage!

God orchestrated for Monty and I to spend time together very much against Monty's will. I took advantage of these times to try to show Monty the 'new' me. The 'at-peace' me. A couple of days before our divorce was to be final, God touched Monty's heart and Monty told his lawyer to stop the divorce.

Here we are five years later, celebrating our twenty-fifth wedding anniversary!

As hard as that time was in my life I would not change it for anything. I needed to wake up so I could really start being a Christ-follower, and to truly and completely give my life to the One who created me. I have learned to "Let go and let God," as the saying goes. I had finally put my total trust in Him and no longer tried to control everything around me. I could live at peace with myself and others.

The enemy tries hard to pull me back into that old lifestyle. I know the only way to stay out of it is to stay in the Word and walk closely with God. I am happier and more content now than I have ever been. I am excited to see what God has in store for us!

See That He Is Good

Monty Jensen

*M*uch like many of you, I grew up in a traditional American home—mom, dad, siblings, pets—attending school and sadly, only occasionally attending church. Most church attendance was on major holidays. Unlike the majority of the country, I spent most of my early years on our family's ranches and farms. Many of you know of the maturing experiences gained by this lifestyle and I am thankful that I had that opportunity . . . or thankful for at least part of it.

There are some basic aspects of ranch life that distinguish it from any other lifestyle or job, like daylight to dark work days, working where you live and living where you work, total commitment to the lifestyle, not just a job and the least favorite of all, the inconsistency of income. It all makes it what it is. To some of us that's okay, but to some, like my mother, these were the most unfavorable conditions one could ever be expected to live under. She resented my dad and my paternal grandparents for *forcing* her to leave the city life and luxury she had enjoyed.

I had no clue that this was such a point of contention in my parents' life until I was fourteen. It all blew up on my mom's thirtieth birthday. My dad had spent the last year building a huge ranch-style dream home—the home that my mom wanted. It was almost complete; almost a reality, but the carpenter my dad had hired to help build it disappeared with my mom in the middle of the night. The carpenter left a wife and two children, and my mom left behind my dad, four sons and the lifestyle that she never wanted.

I found myself being both a big brother and a mom to my three younger brothers. I already had chores to do every morning and night, but now I had the added responsibilities of getting my brothers dressed, making lunches, collecting books and homework for school. We had to be on the bus by 5:45 every morning, and back on the bus after school to return each night at 5:05. Dad still had the place to run so it was left up to me to help make life happen. It was months before we ever heard from my mother.

I didn't fully realize it for many years, but I resented her terribly for abandoning us all. Eventually my dad remarried, but it was to an unpleasant woman who had four children of her own. Her kids were spoiled, defiant, undisciplined little brats. My brothers all went to live with my mom and when I was sixteen I left home to go live with my grandparents to help run their farm and to care for them as they aged.

When I was a junior in high school I enlisted in the Army Guard, and when I turned eighteen I transferred to the regular Army, leaving for what I believed would likely be a career. Things were lonely for me, but it was there that I got my first taste of a church that was much different from what I had ever experienced. I remember being given many opportunities to 'accept Christ as my Lord and Savior' but never felt like I knew what to do with it.

After suffering an injury that would ultimately send me home, I went through a period of terrible depression and feeling of uselessness. My mom didn't want me, the Army now had no use for me, and I knew if I failed here that my dad and grandfather would both be terribly disappointed in me.

I was a fourth-generation Army soldier and I was expected to accomplish at least what generations before me had accomplished. I realized that because of my circumstances pleasing my father and grandfather was a near impossibility. I had spent my entire life trying to do just that. I returned home to my grandparents' farm hoping for acceptance but relatively sure I would be ridiculed and reassured of my worthlessness.

Shortly after returning home I got involved with the men's vocal ensemble at my grandparents' church and found that I had something special. Though not the most accomplished singer, I fit into the group well and I actually enjoyed it. What a gift! I had just received a measure of the acceptance that I was so desperately seeking from this group of men.

Some of the other men in the group were not your traditional 'Sunday-only Christians.' I came to hear of Bible studies that many of them were attending and felt a little intrigued. I began to attend some of these Bible studies and began reading the Bible on my own. I came to believe that I had as much access to Jesus and His forgiveness as any priest or pastor did and that I could pray directly to Jesus and not have to go through any mediator to get through to Him: not a priest, a pastor, or any of the saints, or even the Virgin Mary herself! This was mind-blowing to me!

A small group of us went to visit our local priest one afternoon with hopes of getting some clarification on some of the issues we felt we were facing. The priest listened to us for a short time and responded only with *you boys are reading the Bible too much*. Now I was really interested! However, when the priest made my grandfather aware of the extent of my involvement in this 'blasphemous activity' of Bible reading, I was no longer allowed to 'conspire with these rebels.'

In the spring of 1986 while at a Saturday evening mass I, was singing with the men's group when the young lady I now call my bride attended with a friend. The young woman she came with was a friend of one of the other men in the group. As it turns out, she asked her friend about me, I asked my friend about her and, well, apparently music has more to offer than one may think!

I learned of her failed marriage and eminent divorce, her refusal to be bullied and her commitment to her sons' welfare and happiness. As we got to know one another better, we struggled through some disagreements but also enjoyed many hours of laughter. Both of us knew that a commitment was necessary.

In the fall during our courtship, we heard of a Lowell Lundstrum crusade that was going on in a town about an hour and a half away. Some encouragement from her sister and brother-in-law and our curiosity lead us to the event that would be a defining factor in my future and my acceptance of Christ.

In January of 1987 I married my wife and her son. Yes—her son—who for months had already been calling me *Dad!* In February we got pregnant with our daughter. This in and of itself was a "God thing," as Sharon was quite sick during most of her first pregnancy and was insistent that she would not have any more children. She had also been using birth control. November came and we shared in the joy of our daughter's birth. Over the next several years we did what all families do: we attended PTA meetings, sporting events, proms and graduations. We reared our children the best way we knew how.

As a couple we struggled with control and power issues. I refused to fight but knew I was to lead my family. My wife refused to let me lead and maintained control in defense of the fears she faced from her childhood. All our married years I felt like I gave all I had to give and felt the nurturing and support was not returned. At one point I held down one full time and two part time jobs just trying to give us a better life.

The full time job though, was as a police officer. The tests and trials that come with public service were hurting us and caused much pain in our marriage and family. Some of our church family at the time even got involved in the painful rumors and malice. We separated ourselves from church, church people and God for several years.

After our daughter graduated and moved out, I told Sharon that we were done and I couldn't live like we had been. Honestly, I was quite mean and insensitive through it all and I felt justified. This was terribly uncharacteristic for me but I felt the need to begin taking care of *me*.

During our separation, we both found that that God was right there waiting for us, but in very different ways. I was working then as a construction superintendent, and my hours were long and the responsibilities many. Of the tradesmen who worked for me, one was a jail-house convert, biker, and born-again Christian who God had planted in my life for just a time as this. As he heard of my life struggles and recent separation from my wife, he made it known to me that he was a Christian and that he would like to talk to me. He told me that he and his wife were going to be praying that God would heal our marriage. I assured him I had no use for the God I had seen in action in my past and even less did I want my marriage healed. He left well enough alone, at least till the next day. This man literally had to fear for his job, as I had control over whether he had work or he didn't, but, thankfully, he was relentless in this pursuit of scriptural justice.

Sharon's older brother and sister-in-law lived very near us and had become quite close. They too were devout Christians and insisted on reminding me that there was a much bigger God than my obstacles were. Even worse, for me at least, their home is where Sharon lived during our separation. I tried (God knows I tried) to emotionally an spiritually remove myself from her and our relationship as I had done physically. Throughout the next three months, Sharon, her brother Doug and Cody, as well as the carpenter on my job continued to leave voice mails and letters in the mail trying to get me to see the injustice in all of this.

Sharon had started seeing a counselor and was making great strides in changing who she had allowed herself to become and would try to get me to see that she wanted to make it better. She wanted me to know that she had found God again through it all. *Great—that's all I need, to have another lashing from the whip of this God that's supposed to love me and wants the best for me.* I couldn't see it and didn't want to try. I was going to be *me* now, not what *she* wanted me to be.

Well, as fate, (or God) would have it, I felt a softening of heart and a release from *me* to spend time with Cody and his wife over dinner. After several conversations with them, I agreed to a challenge they placed before me. They said: *Test him—test God and see that He is good.* They knew my birthday was coming, and they suggested that if I didn't have an undeniable conviction and direction for my life *without* Sharon by my birthday, that I should give God and Sharon the opportunity to be a part of my life.

I laid in bed that night crying and telling God how I ould never go back to where I was. All I got back was, *No can't.* The next day I called Sharon to ask if she would consider moving home. I think there was some hesitation but it was never evident. All of this was years ago. Today we can say that by the grace of God we have survived the enemy's test and have recently celebrated twenty-five years of marriage. We are looking forward to at least that many more.

"Expand on where you are with God today, ministries you are involved with
. . . the hope you have for the future."

Always Enough

Sharon Taylor

To begin, you can say that I am an authentic 'Greenie.' I was born and raised in Fort Collins, Colorado. Both of my parents drank and fought verbally and physically all the time. They were not Christians. All the time I was growing up, I never knew which dad was coming home from work. Would it be the drunk one or the sober one? To this day, I can't remember a time when my parents ever told me that they loved me. All I remember are the fights, the name-calling and the cussing.

I had a dear friend that I had met before I started school. She and her family introduced me to their church, which was called The Salvation Army Church. They would be sure the bus stopped at our house to pick me up for Sunday school. I was involved in the youth programs but I had never made a commitment to Jesus Christ. I went to church whenever I could to escape the chaos at home. I spent a lot of time at my friend's home and learned what a normal family was like.

I was wild as a teenager and began drinking and looking for love in all the wrong places. I got married the first time when I was seventeen just to get out of the house. That was one of the biggest mistakes of my life. My husband was an abuser, and the marriage ended in divorce after two years. My parents divorced about the same time.

I moved to Denver and met my second husband. We married and had a son, and we had a good life. My husband was a decent man and a good father, but even though I had a family and a husband who loved me, I felt that there was something missing in my life.

I began attending the church that I had gone to with my friend and her family when I was just a child. There, I found what I had been looking for and gave my life to God. He filled that hole in my heart that I was trying to fill with all the wrong things. Because of the prayers of my best friend, Maxine, I found what I was looking for. I came to believe that all of us have a place only God can fill, and we waste too much time and go through too much pain in an attempt to fill that hole with everything but God.

I prayed fervently for my husband for years. He didn't mind that I went to church and took our son but he didn't want me preaching at him, and he wanted no part of God.

Years later my in-laws were living with us when my father-in-law developed cancer and passed away. This was very hard on my husband because he was very close to his dad, and my mother-in-law detested me. After her husband's death, her hatred became even more evident. It was only Christ that sustained me during that difficult time. The emotional abuse that she laid on me still affects me to this day. Finally my mother-in-law moved out.

Be careful of your words, for they can destroy a person.

My husband needed answers, refuge and peace, so he began attending church with me. After thirteen years, God answered my prayers and my husband came to know Jesus Christ as his personal Lord and Savior. We became very involved in the church and our church family was very close. Never quit praying for someone!

Throughout my married life I worked off and on as needed. I worked as a waitress for a number of years and then as secretary / bookkeeper for The Salvation Army Church for about ten years. Shortly after we had celebrated our thirtieth wedding anniversary my husband became very ill. By the time the doctors figured out that he had leukemia it was too late, and he went home to be with his Lord. My world as I knew it came crashing down. This is when I truly found out that *if Jesus was all you had would He be enough*?

The answer is a resounding *YES*! My church was there to support me during this difficult time in my life.

I had worked with Dick years before when he was the Kettle Coordinator for The Salvation Army where I was working. My pastor had asked me to work during the Christmas season to help with the toy distribution, and while I was at work one day, Dick called to see if we had any extra toys for a family here in Douglas. I invited him to call and we would go have coffee and visit the next time he was in town.

I was surprised when Dick called a few months later. He came by to visit and when he left my roommate told me *you two are going to be together.* I laughed at her and told her *I'm not moving to Douglas, Wyoming.* She just smiled at me. *Don't tell God what you will or will not do!* Here I am!

I had not been looking for a husband but God put a Christian man in my life. God knew, those years before, that Dick and I would be together. Nothing surprises Him. We dated and got married. I went from having one child to six, and from no grandchildren to four (that one was kind of hard)! We now have eleven beautiful grandchildren. Coming from the big city (Denver) I didn't know how I would adjust to small town living but come to find out God, in His infinite wisdom, knew I would love it.

About three years ago Dick and I were looking for a church home. We came to The Gathering and when I walked in the doors I felt like I was at home. As you probably already guessed, Dick is the social butterfly of the family. I am basically shy and reserved, and it's hard for me to step out of my 'comfort zone.'

God has led Dick and I to CMA (Christian Motorcycle Association). When we go to the rallies and other events we have the opportunity to share the love of Christ. This is way out of my comfort zone but God wants me to grow, so it's in His strength that I go.

I have found out that Jesus is really all I need and that He loves me as I am. I don't need the approval of anyone but my Lord and Savior. There's a song I use to sing in Sunday school:

He's still working on me, to make me what I ought to be.
It took Him just a week to make the Moon and Stars,
The Sun and the Earth and Jupiter and Mars.
How loving and patient He must be,
He's still working on me.

Never An Accident

Dick Taylor

I was born in Nebraska, but have been in Wyoming most of my life. My family moved around quite a bit and I lived in fourteen different towns by the time I was four years old. We finally moved to Lander. I grew up and attended school there.

I went to church for years when I was a child but the only thing I knew was that Jesus was coming back someday. I thought that He would be born all over again, grow up, and just 'be here.' To me, the Bible was a very difficult book and that last chapter, "The Concordance" seemed really weird!

Just before I turned seventeen, my folks divorced. That was a big blow to me. Being seventeen, I was able to choose who I wanted to live with, and I chose to live with my dad in Jeffery City. He taught me all the things I needed to know to be a man: how to drink, cuss, smoke, and treat women as sex objects.

He taught me good things too. I was raised by the 'Code of the West—The Cowboy Ethics' that Jim Anderson spoke about in his message at The Gathering earlier in 2011. During that time dad was going through some bad times of his own, but all in all my father was a great dad.

I had a car wreck that could have killed me in my senior year of high school. It broke my pelvis in four places and I spent a month in the hospital. I firmly believe that this was one of God's attempts to get my attention, but of course I wasn't listening.

I began to run around with the wrong crowd. We would party and sometimes the drinking would lead to getting into trouble. One night I was with a couple of guys who stole a pair of motorcycles from a private residence and we went riding in the hills. Another time, six of us were riding around drinking when the driver pulled up to an underground mine entrance. He went in and came out with some dynamite and fuses. We went around trying to blow up stuff, (out of town of course). Eventually we got caught and I had to pay a hefty fine and spent six months on probation.

I got married to my girlfriend right after she graduated from high school. My first marriage only lasted four years. We had a daughter and then my wife left me for someone else.

I did a lot of drinking in those days—mainly partying with my friends or playing pool for beer. I smoked a little marijuana. One time I was car-pooling from work with four other guys when one of them pulled out a joint and we passed it around. By the time we reached the parking lot my heart was beating about 200 bpm. It lasted for over a half an hour and scared me to death. I didn't dare go to the doctor. That was the last time I smoked marijuana!

My mom went to church out of conviction and my dad went because it was the 'thing to do' back then. Mom had always said she was a Christian but I didn't believe it because I thought for a person to be a Christian you had to be perfect. My mom was not perfect. When my parents divorced I turned away from the church. The only time I was ever in a church was for weddings and funerals until I was twenty-nine years old.

By this time my second wife and I had three sons. I was working at a good job but my wife felt that the kids needed to go to church. She started looking around for a church that felt right for the family. We were living in Shirley Basin, Wyoming, a small mining town of less than a thousand people and very few churches. She ended up going to the Shirley Basin Baptist Church and came to know the Lord. When she told me about it I said, "That's fine for you, just don't preach to me. I am going to Hell and proud of it."

Well, the Lord had a different plan.

It was a couple of months later that the church was having a revival. My wife had asked me all week if I would go with her, but I was always too tired after work (at least that was my excuse)! Then that Friday at work my conscience kept telling me to go to church with her. I was thinking that wouldn't hurt me and it would get her off my back.

When I got home that night I was surprised to see that she wasn't ready to go to church. I asked her why and she told me that she wasn't feeling well. I told her that was too bad because I had thought about going to church with her that night. She felt better instantly!

That night, for the first time in my life, I came to the realization of who Christ really was. I heard about the forgiveness of Christ, and how He would forgive me of all my sins. After the service I walked up to Ed, the pastor and told him I was 'ready.'

I prayed that night for forgiveness and asked Christ to become my Lord and Savior. *AND HE DID.* Ever since that night my life has been changed—not perfect by any means, but a whole lot better. My language changed as did my outlook on life. My thought patterns changed. I felt like I had a purpose in life—not just wandering aimlessly. I quit drinking and smoking.

I was so hungry for the things of God that I was in church anytime there was a service. Within about a year I was the youth teacher and treasurer of our little church. I found out that one way to really learn about God and His Word is to become a teacher. You have to study because some of those kids, especially the youth, were pretty smart.

When that job ended I moved to Hanna, Wyoming where we had a growing church with all kinds of studies going on. I got involved with our church association as youth and camp director.

During that time we were in Shirley Basin, I had felt the calling to go into the ministry, and when the mine shut down in Hanna we moved to the Denver area so I could attend Colorado Christian University. We found a really good church in Brighton that we attended for about seven years. I graduated from CCU with a diploma in Theology but I never pursued getting a church of my own because of a lack of support from my wife.

I kept on teaching in church: middle school, youth and adults. I spent the last four years in Colorado working a second job at Christmas time for the Salvation Army, helping with the canteen during disasters, and running their Kettle Campaign in the Englewood area.

Eventually we moved to Douglas where I went to work at the coal mine. I worked there for almost eleven years. Then my back gave out. I am now on disability and retired from the mine.

When we moved here we joined a local church where I taught youth for years and was involved in all aspects of the church. My wife was involved too, until she decided to quit going. She finally left after twenty-six and a half years of marriage. We had four boys. She went through the change of life and the 'empty nest syndrome,' and finally left me. That was a very hard time, but the thing I did **not** do was turn my back on God and His people—that's where I found my greatest source of comfort.

After two years, through a variety of circumstances, I got in contact with Sharon, who I had known for twelve years. We had worked together for the Salvation Army in Colorado. I was also acquainted with her late husband and their son. Sharon and I soon got together, dated and then married. A country song states it perfectly:

> *It was no accident me finding you,*
> *Someone had a hand in it,*
> *Long before we ever knew.*
> *Now I just can't believe you're in my life*
> *Heaven's smilin' down on me . . .*
> *I tip my hat to the keeper of the stars,*
> *He sure knew what he was doin',*
> *When he joined these two hearts . . ."*

Sharon and I attended various churches until we started coming to The Gathering almost three years ago. Although I had been involved in many different ministries, I find that the Christian Motorcyclists Association has become my main ministry. I love to ride and I love to talk to people about Jesus. I feel that is where the Lord wants me.

I could list all the things I have done for Christ over the years but it is what the Lord has done *for* me and **through** me that is important. The Lord has been great to me, and even when I have sinned against Him, He has not forsaken me. When I struggled with throat cancer a couple of years ago, I never blamed Him nor did I abandon Him because He has never left my side.

When I was about eight years old I learned a verse that has stayed with me all my life: *"And he brought them out, and said, Sirs, what must I do to be saved? And they said, Believe on the Lord Jesus Christ, and thou shalt be saved, and thy house."* Acts 16:30-31.

Spiritually Discerned

Liz Bartos

This story is not really about me. Being seventy-five years old I probably have much to say, but this story is about the faithfulness and goodness of God in my life.

My mother was a single mom and in 1946 there were few, if any, day care centers. When I was nine years old, she placed me in a Christian Chinese Girls Home. This began to build a foundation for me. When I was twelve years old I attended a summer camp, and accepted the invitation to receive Jesus as my Lord and Savior. When I did, I felt an overwhelming warmth and love and peace embrace me. However, that wonderful feeling eventually faded. I went to live with my mother when I turned fourteen. She didn't attend church, and my Christian walk was interrupted.

Over the years there were times when I was surrounded with God's beautiful creations. Those special times might have been a visit to the seashore or a grand mountaintop, and that wonderful, warm feeling would momentarily return. It would fade once again when I came down from the mountain. My heart longed to permanently recapture that feeling.

When I turned thirty-eight, I was into the fifth year of my second marriage. I was an unhappy, disillusioned, angry wife and mother. My husband was overseas, and I could have cared less if he ever returned. It wasn't good situation—it was a sad and lonely one.

I had two daughters from my previous marriage. One was an adolescent who fought me constantly. I had begun attending church when the children were small, and we were continuing to do so. Somehow I instinctively knew this was the right thing to do, but I wasn't a very good Christian witness to my children nor to anyone else.

Today, I realize that no matter where a person is, God will move heaven and earth to get them where He wants them to be, regardless of their failures. Looking back I see God's hand was orchestrating everything in my life.

At one time I attended a class of "Death and Dying" at my church. The leader broke us up into small groups, and gave us a statement to discuss. The statement was: *I feel dying early will happen to others and not me.* We were to respond with a *'yes'* or a *'no,'* and then discuss the reason. My response was *No!* In the back of my mind I had this fear that if I died, who would be there for my children? The more

I thought about it, the more I came to the realization that I had prepared my children to do many practical things in life, but was negligent on how to cope with life's difficulties. I, for one, was not a very good example. Strange—we attended church every week but never talked about our faith at home. We never spoke about **JESUS!** We never even said His **name** in our home!

Driving home that evening, the awareness both bothered and excited me at the same time. When I got home I found my oldest daughter still up and doing her homework. I was eager to tell her what was on my mind. As I spoke, she didn't respond well . . . not looking at me she began to fidget and even folded a paper airplane and floated it across the room. At first, I began to get irritated at her rudeness and then realized that she wasn't meaning to be rude. She was embarrassed when I openly spoke the name of Jesus. I said it again and the sound of His name resonated through the house.

I placed my hands on both of her shoulders and bent down to look into her face. She looked at the floor and could not look me in the eye. I confessed to her that something was terribly wrong in our life, but I promised that things would be different from now on. I didn't know what or how.

Two weeks later a friend invited me to attend a week-long Discipleship Seminar at our church. **Whoa!** I thought . . . *a whole week at church?* It was all I could to do go for one day, but a whole week? Nevertheless, at her insistence, I agreed to go the first night.

After the introduction they broke us in to small groups. Our leader, a young man in what I imagined to be in his twenties or early thirties made the statement, "For many years I thought I was a Christian, but I was not."

I wanted to ask him *what do you mean and how do you know?* But I felt it was a stupid question since all of us going to a Christian church had to be Christians. An older man to my left, God bless him, asked the question I wanted to ask. He began speaking about having a 'personal relationship' with Jesus Christ. I didn't have a clue what he was talking about, but there was something sincere and humble about the testimony he gave. It spoke to my heart. Consequently, I stayed that week and went every single night. There was something wholesome and 'normal' about this group of people! I was drawn to them. They didn't act austere nor did they dress funny. They smiled and laughed. They were **normal** yet possessed something that I did **not** have. I saw joy, warmth, graciousness and a humble confidence in God.

As it turned out, after their leader gave the final Sunday morning message he had an altar call. I was propelled up to the altar by some unseen force. I was sobbing all the way—literally—uncontrollably sobbing. I was so embarrassed but I couldn't stop. I wasn't sure why I was up there. I was so broken and hurting over my failures: two marriages, hurting children, being angry and disillusioned. I made no verbal confession to God, nor did I make any promises. I did not say a sinner's prayer, but I believe God read my heart and His Holy Spirit came into my life right at that moment!

Incredibly, that feeling I once experienced at summer camp when I was twelve years old was back, and this time it stayed. I felt totally loved by God and I was crazy about Him. I began to read the Bible and what used to be so boring suddenly came alive. I couldn't get enough of it. I was so hungry!

In my enthusiasm I did some crazy things which today, when I think back, embarrass me tremendously. After all those years of being in bondage to sin, finally being so totally loved by God—the freedom I felt was exhilarating! Baby Christians often go off half-whacked, and that I did!

First, I wrote my husband, still overseas, and told him about my 'new love,' Jesus. It scared him half to death! He was totally threatened and thought that I had gone off the deep end—perhaps even standing on street corners, witnessing, or going door to door.

When he arrived home I was determined that things would be different. Jesus was in my life, and we would all become a wonderful Christian family and all go to heaven together. 'I' would make sure that would happen, right? *No, not so fast!* I proceeded to work out 'MY' strategy, as silly as it seems now.

- I put scripture notes in sandwiches he took to work.
- I left Christian books open all around the house.
- I constantly (and loudly) played Christian music.
- I prodded him into going to numerous Christian functions.
- I put great pressure on him to change.

I was too immature in my Christian faith to know scripture well, especially 1 Corinthians 1:14 which states "Natural man CANNOT know the things of the spirit for they are spiritually discerned."

I was trying to make my husband into something he was unable to be. Bless his soul, he is a man of integrity and just won't pretend to be something that he's not. He had no Holy Spirit to lead and guide him As a result, he began to get angrier and angrier. Rather than see our marriage getting better, it got worse. I couldn't understand because I had become so 'holy and righteous.' (More like self-righteous!)

I did, however, begin to grow in my faith. Much of it came by trial and error, and God's grace and guidance. One morning during my 'quiet time' I was praying for my husband, and God spoke to my heart and asked me a very direct question. *Why do you want "D" saved?*

I began to list all the reasons I could think of:

- I wanted someone to share my faith and go to church with me.
- I wanted someone to pray with.
- I wanted a Christian father for my children.
- I wanted—I wanted—I wanted . . .

All seemed valid and good reasons, but God showed me that everything started with 'I.' It was all about *me* and had nothing to do with my husband going to heaven or hell. God showed me that I was praying with a wrong heart and wrong motives.

Again, God spoke to my heart. *If I choose to save him with his last breath, can you love him just the way he is*? No strings attached. Wow! That was an eye *and* a heart opener. I knew, as zealous as I was, it would take God and His grace to make this happen. I proposed to relax and trust God and I made a decision. *Yes, I will try.*

God showed me the message getting to my husband was not one of love and acceptance (1 Corinthians 13:love). It was a message that he was good enough *before* I was a Christian and now that I *was* a Christian, he was no longer acceptable and *he* needed to change. (Not me, of course!)

God showed me that I was not called to change another person. That was His job. My job was to love them. I could only change myself, and even then, it would only be possible with His help.

My decision was the turning point in our marriage and because of it, I began a closer walk with God. God most often will use the difficult things in our life to 'rub off the rough edges' on us. This was one of those times. God had a lot of work to do on me.

Learning to trust God has been a wonderful journey all these years. A good part of the time it has been two steps forward and one step back, and sometimes vice versa. Growth has been slow at times but I believe that slow growth endures. The way to tell if growth was taking place in my life was to look back to where I was thirty-seven years ago in comparison to where I am today. Throughout the journey I can see God's hand on every situation in my life and I am truly humbled by His love, His grace, and His interest in me. I often think *me?* In the grand scheme of things? ***Who am I, really?*** I am but a speck, but he values and still cares for me! That is awesome!

Bottom line: God is faithful and God is good!

I have come to a personal conclusion that when a person makes a commitment to God, He takes them seriously and will be faithful to complete that work in their life (Philippians 1:6.) God remembered a little twelve-year old girl's decision at summer camp, and He was faithful and never gave up on her!

I have taught Sunday School throughout the years, and I am persuaded of the importance for children to give their hearts to Jesus when they are small, a time when their hearts are still soft. They may not totally understand, but God does. He honors and takes them at their word and He sees into their heart. He is faithful!

Be encouraged regarding loved ones—God will complete the work that he began in their lives! Though they may stray He will never rest until His will is done! Acts 16:31 says "Believe in the Lord Jesus Christ and you will be saved. You and your household."

"For this is good and acceptable in the sight of God our Savior who desires all men to be saved and come to the knowledge of truth." (1 Timothy 2:4-5)

God saved me. He saved my marriage. I am trusting that he will save my dear husband of forty-two years.

Even with his last breath—you bet! . . . If that is what it will take
My job? To just love . . . with the love of Jesus in me
To keep praying and keep trusting God
Because His grace is always sufficient.

The Mighty Hands Of God

Francis J. Horn

I was raised on a small farm in South Dakota, with five brothers and one sister. We survived on a low income with just the basics of food clothing, and shelter. Dad would often go to town and come home drunk. When he was drinking he would become very abusive. Many nights we spent at the neighbor's or in a straw stack to keep warm. During one of these episodes, my father took down a .22 rifle and attempted to shoot my mother. The rifle misfired.

The next morning two of my brothers—with me tagging along—checked on the misfired cartridge. The firing pin had made a dent in the primer. My older brother put the bullet back into the .22 rifle and the gun fired. I thought *Wow!* It made a big impression on me knowing that God could—and did—stop a gun from firing.

A family friend led me to accept Christ as my Lord and Savior in 1972. There was not an immediate change in my attitude or behavior. I drank and partied many more years. In 1984 I stopped drinking . . . almost. I had this idea that I could drink just one drink and stop. I was so wrong: one drink led to another and soon I would be drunk again. Sobriety led to a divorce from my first wife. She told me that she could handle the drinking, but not my behavior when I was sober. Shortly after the divorce God led me to Alanon and then to AA. December 25, 1989, was the last day that I had a drink of alcohol.

The next time that I knew God cared for me happened when I was living in Gillette and driving a propane truck. That winter of 1982 through 1983 it was very cold and snowy. Demand for propane was high so customers could keep their homes warm, and we were working from twelve to fifteen hours a day to keep up with the demand. One night I was coming back to town on the 4-J Road around 10 p.m. I fell asleep at the wheel of my delivery truck, and a hand appeared in front of me pointing toward the barrow pit—where the truck was headed. I managed to get the truck stopped safely and got out of the truck, wondering at the miracle of the hand appearing in time for me to gain control of the truck and avoid a serious accident. I was curious and amazed at the way the hand appeared: it was a left hand with the palm towards me. It made no sense to me until I realized there was a right hand around my shoulder holding me.

Vicki and I were blessed with our son Dusty, on November 17,1994. The pregnancy was a difficult one for Vicki, and she was ordered to bed rest the last fifteen weeks of her pregnancy because of the potential of premature labor. The doctor induced labor, and shortly after they had to do an emergency caesarean section. Vicki's uterus was tearing, and was very close to an artery. The following day the doctor found a blockage in Dusty's heart, a coarctation of the lower artery and a heart murmur. Life Flight was called and they took Dusty to Children's Hospital in Denver. Vicki was unable to go with us. When we arrived in Denver, the doctors ordered an ultrasound on Dusty's heart, and to our surprise the blockage had disappeared. Dusty still has a heart murmur but Vicki and I feel that Dusty is our miracle baby.

In 1997 I was driving from Rapid City to Spearfish on I-90, and I again felt God's divine intervention in my life. I was behind a pickup pulling a stock trailer filled with cows. I was about to pass the pickup and trailer when it suddenly started to sway back and forth. The trailer was loaded too heavy in the back, making it light on the hitch of the pickup. Just as I was about to pass the trailer, I felt a presence telling me that it wasn't safe to pass. Just as I stepped on the brakes, the driver of the pickup lost control and jack-knifed the trailer in my lane, going into the center median. The stock trailer rolled and ejected a cow out of the trailer. If I had not stepped on the brakes I would have been in between the pickup and the stock trailer.

In the much-loved piece entitled "Footprints in the Sand," the picture of the footprints and what they represent is how I feel when I think about how God has carried me many times in my life. I feel humbled to know beyond any doubt that God has worked many miracles in my life, protecting me and my family. Disbelievers say God is dead. I know beyond any doubt that God is alive, and still doing miracles!

What is next? God has led me to tell my story and to write a book about my life and its experiences. Even though I don't consider myself a writer, with God's help and prayer I hope someday to write that book.